MOLEFI KETE ASANTE

Kemet, Afrocentricity and Knowledge

Africa World Press, Inc.

P.O. Box 1892
Trenton, New Jersey 08607

Africa World Press, Inc.

P.O. Box 1892
Trenton, New Jersey 08607

First Printing, 1990
Second Printing, January 1992
Third Printing, May 1992

Cover design by Ife Nii Owoo

Book design and electronic typesetting from author's disk by
Malcolm Litchfield
This book is composed in Sabon and Optima Bold

Library of Congress Catalog Card Number: 90-82735

ISBN: 0-86543-188-4   Cloth
           0-86543-189-2   Paper

CONTENTS

PREFACE

My intellectual debts are extensive in regards to the ideas in this book. I have read Thuthmosis III, Ptahhotep, Amenomope, Ogotommeli, Delaney, Blyden, Garvey, Du Bois, and groups of European thinkers such as Platonists, Aristotelians, especially the Neo-Aristotelians, Hegelians, Marxists, and Wittgensteinians. However, I am most keenly a Diopian, believing essentially that Cheikh Anta Diop has said quite enough on the theories of culture and history to inform most of what I write. Those whose works I do not mention or whose names I do not call but to whom I am indebted are equally my teachers. More particularly, of the contemporary theorists, I am most closely associated with the intellectual circle expounded by the philosopher Maulana Karenga and the scientist Wade Nobles whose works are essentially analytical and critical in much the same way as mine.

Scientificalism may or may not be based on originality but the idea of an Afrocentric method is to demonstrate its capability and flexibility with a range of possible questions in an original manner. By science, however, I do not mean merely the steps of the so-called scientific method but rather the proper attitude toward imagination and creation. Various traditions may be used to assist in creating the new but it is in the originality of the particular idea that one sets himself or herself apart from the previous traditions. The Afrocentric method seeks to transform human reality by ushering in a human openness to cultural pluralism which cannot exist without the unlocking of the minds for acceptance of an expansion of consciousness. I seek to overthrow parochialism, provincialism, and narrow Wotanic visions of the world by demonstrating the usefulness of an Afrocentric approach to questions of knowledge.

There is nothing profound in such a pronouncement, there have been similar pronouncements by various other writers, but what is different is the identification of the principal cause of the failure in those other formulations. The major problem with existentialism, phenomenology, and structuralism, for example, is that they have hedged their bets in a European worldview that is moribund when it comes to looking at the outside world. *They cannot truly grasp the significance of a revolutionary idea that would change the European method itself.* There are several reasons for this state of affairs. The first is that they would be overturning themselves, a most difficult task, particularly if they believe that there is at least a little bit of good in their formulation. Secondly we are talking to and about a society or worldview that has dominated for 500 years. What would the philosophers of Europe mean by humanism except perhaps expanding to other Europeans, except perhaps to admit other peoples into the historical consciousness of Europe? But for Europeans to enter into a view, a perspective where they will be able to share with others in a world of plural perspectives is to ask them to submit to revolution. But it is not so bad. In fact, it is a realism that must come in order to protect the Eurocentric view as a human view. All around the globe the exclusive Eurocentric view is called into question by those who have finally gained their own footing. There is a growing critique of hegemony and domination. No one will be a slave anymore. The former slaves are using every means possible to maintain their revolt against oppression; and in revolt, they overturn both their own victimization and oppression. But the project of human knowledge is even more, it is a search for method that will establish a base for further inquiry into the processes and practices of human culture. Afrocentricity, as an aspect of centrism, is groundedness which allows the student of human culture investigating African phenomena to view the world from the standpoint of the African.

I have divided the book into three sections: (1) interiors, (2) anteriors, and (3) exteriors. The idea is to examine what constitutes the discipline of Africalogy; secondly, a discussion of origins and issues related to historical developments in the writing of Africa; and thirdly, a presentation of approaches to fields other than Africalogy with particular emphasis on critique. The idea for such a division was first suggested to me after reading the work of Cheikh Anta Diop on the Egyptian anteriority in African languages. I hope that I have not complicated matters for my readers.

I present this volume as an offering to Jehuty; may it be accepted as a small token of gratitude for having passed this way.

ACKNOWLEDGEMENTS

An ancient African proverb from the Nile Valley says, "I am a king by nature, a ruler to whom one does not have to give." It is in the spirit of the richness, the abundance of African and African American culture that I offer this volume. I suppose it is in some senses what Houston Baker calls an "anti-book book or a non-book book" inasmuch as it confronts oppressive discourse. But it is not intended to be anything more or less than one person's earnest attempt to provide a sense of clarity around the field that is now being called Africalogy. Several colleagues, many of them in my own department, have been exceedingly helpful in the formulation of my ideas. I have often given thanks to Amon for surrounding me with colleagues who are genuinely friends, brothers and sisters, whose questions and comments and criticisms, while frequently stinging, do have healing properties. Kariamu Welsh Asante, C. Tsehloane Keto, Stella Hargett, Thelma Ravell-Pinto, Daudi Azibo, Sonja Peterson-Lewis, Charles Fuller, Alfred Moleah, and James Ravell have all assisted me in this project one way or another. I have also learned from Nilgün Okur of Ege University, Izmir, Turkey, who spent a Fulbright year in our department.

I have used the resources of the Charles Blockson Afro-American Collection and the Paley Library at Temple University. In addition, the Director of the University Libraries, James Myers, has graciously extended to me the use of a small study room to that I can occasionally escape the constant ringing of my office telephone. For this service, I am especially grateful.

It is most difficult to think of the proper appreciation for those without whom the technical aspects of this book could never have been achieved. Yet I shall to try to convey my sincere gratitude to Nadia Kravchenko, who goes from victory to victory on the computer and Debi Tillman, who directs a host of characters in the department by simply saying, thank you very much. My publisher and friend, Kassahun Checole, continues to express faith in my project.

This book would never have appeared were it not for the critique and debate of the first doctoral students in African American Studies at Temple University. The "thirty five" are not only brilliant and enthusiastic but they are thoughtful and reflective. Alongside my son, Molefi Khumalo, whom they have all adopted, I dedicate this book to them.

PART I

INTERIORS _____

Intellectual Landscapes

C ornel West has written in *Prophetic Fragments* that "we live in a time of cultural disarray and social decay, an age filled with ruins and fragments. Hence, our intellectual landscapes are littered with allegorical tales of deterioration rather than dramative narratives of reconciliation."[1] While I would not go quite so far as West to bemoan the contemporary intellectual landscape, there is no escaping the fact that few offers of illuminating dramas are presented for review. But circumstances such as described by West alone present fruitful times and like the ancient Africans who lived along the banks of the Nile who took advantage of whatever situation was presented to them by the river's flow, we must take full advantage of the allegorical conditions found in our societies. If the river was full of water, the Egyptians used large barges to float stones to various sites. If the river had little water, they used heavy sledges pulled by hundreds of people over constantly replaced wooden rollers.

The terrible intellectual plight of the Western world is often laid at the feet of the positivists. Surely the charge, while probably having some truth, is overrated. As a philosophical position, worked out by Saint-Simon and August Comte in the nineteenth century and carried out in the projects of the empiricists and logical positivists in the twentieth century, positivism meant simply that which is given and has to be accepted as it is found rather than going beyond to something unknown such as had been the case in some theological and metaphysical circles. The appeal of the positivist program is its commitment to a hard-headed, no-nonsense interpretation of reality. By setting up the basis for logical positivism with its verifiability tests and by extending the empiricist vision, positivism has insinuated itself into every form of modern Western thought. The logical positivists, particularly of the Vienna Circle in the 1920s and 1930s, tried to systematize empiricism's search for experience by suggesting that propositions might not be false or true but meaningful or meaningless depending upon whether or not they could be verified by observation. The West, as the principal source and receiver of this philosophical view, has succumbed in many of its institutions to a rather materialist conception of reality.

Positivism has brought us to a highly technically managed and structured society where all knowledge flows upward to more efficiently control and dominate society. We are either locked in or shut out; the only action expected of us is to adapt to the situation in the name of structural necessity, rational efficiency, and technical progress. The ruling ideologies continue to abuse positions of power on questions of knowledge. That is why I have maintained that the Eurocentric West is trapped, even in its best intentions, by its concentration on itself, its selfishness, its inability to draw a wider picture. Thus it becomes possible for Trent Schroyer writing in *The Critique of Domination* to begin his attack on a scientized Western civilization with a passage such as the following:

> The critique of domination, or the reflective critique of socially unnecessary constraints of human freedom, is as old as the Western concept of reason. In classical Greek philosophy the notion of reason (*nous*) was developed in relation to the "seeing" of the invisible in the visible, or of the essential in the appearing. For example, in Plato's famous cave allegory the painful re-turning to the sun (i.e., beauty, truth) involved a recognition of the mystifications and domination of conventions (*nomos*) over man's potentialities.[2]

Schroyer's emphasis on the Greeks, who were intellectual children of the Africans, suggests why the Afrocentric method has another advantage over the critical theorists. Wilden, Habermas, Sartre, Marcuse, and other Eurocentricists have tried to work out a critical theory with its ties firmly rooted in the Greek tradition. But I am loosed from that tradition. I claim it as a part of my intellectual heritage but since I share other classical traditions as well I have no reason to be trapped in the European past. Essentially Sartre and Marcuse found that the foundations of a critical theory associated with the concept of negative reason, that is, the knowledge of something because you know what is not, were elusive. My claim is one of freedom from the constraints of Eurocentricists in connection with critical theory; yet I do not claim that the final emancipatory moment will have come when I am finished. The time being, I think that we are on a different road. Stepping outside of the historical moment might permit new interpretations, new criticisms, ultimately the acquisition of new knowledge.

Inside Place

However, one steps outside one's history with great difficulty. In fact, the act itself is highly improbable from true historical consciousness. There is no antiplace, since we are all consumers of space and time. There is, of course, the unknown that we presume is "out there" until we know it by "being there." Our place is the constantly presenting and re-presenting context, the evolving presentation context, the perspective—that is, history to us.

The Afrocentrist sees knowledge of this "place" perspective as a fundamental rule of intellectual inquiry because its content is a self-conscious obliteration of the subject/object duality and the enthronement of an African wholism. A rigorous discipline is necessary to advance the intellectual movement toward a meaningful concept of place. In saying this I am challenging the Afrocentrist to maintain inquiry rooted in a strict interpretation of place in order to betray all naive racial theories and establish Afrocentricity as a legitimate response to the human conditions. All knowledge results from an occasion of encounter in place. But the place remains a rightly shaped perspective that allows the Afrocentrist to put African ideals and values at the center of inquiry. If this does not happen then Afrocentricity does not exist. What are African ideals and values? The answers to this question provide the arena for Afrocentric debate, discussion, and *endarkening*. The Afrocentrist will not question the idea of the centrality of African ideals and values but will argue over what constitutes those ideals and values. The Afrocentrist seeks to uncover and use codes, paradigms, symbols, motifs, myths, and circles of discussion that reinforce the centrality of African ideals and values as a valid frame of reference for acquiring and examining data. Such a method appears to go beyond western history in order to re-valorize the African place in the interpretation of Africans, continental and diasporan.

A collection of data, for example, for an Afrocentric project will consider cognitive and material systems, direct and indirect data—gathering measures, myths, tape or video-recorded conversations, and unobtrusive acquisition processes based on the African culture, e.g., the style of male address used in fervent greetings. Knowledge relates ultimately to some human interest even if it is only to "see" the person who conceives of a problem.

The Africanist Question

Africanists, much like Egyptologists, their counterparts who deal with ancient Egypt, tend to be Europeans whose interest in Africa serves European studies. Where Africans participate in such enterprises, for example, under the aegis of the African Studies Association, they are bound by the same protocols as the European scholars. At the 1988 African Studies Association conference held in Chicago, Illinois, not one panel dealt with (Egyptian) Kemetic traditions or the relationship of the Kemetic culture to the rest of Africa. One asks, how can you have hundreds of scholars participating in an intellectual conference on Africa and no one discusses ancient Egypt or Nubia? During the same week that the African Studies Association was meeting, the American Studies Association met in Miami. The latter conference had numerous panels and papers that referred to the Greeks and Romans.

What many scholars who participate in African Studies do is not properly African Studies but European studies of Africa. This has little to do with the racial background of the scholar but rather with the perspective from which the person examines data. On many trains half of the seats face the direction of travel and half face the opposite direction. You may ride with your back to the direction of travel or in the normal direction with your face facing forward. Although you are moving in one direction, depending upon which way you are faced you get a different view of reality. In the face forward position you see things going. On some trains they have seats against the sides of the wall—in those cases you see things coming and going. Well, we are like that at this moment in history we see things from both vantage points—coming and going—and what we see going are the vestiges of a system of racial domination—it was a wrong headed system in the first place—what we see coming is a post-modern society that is sympathetic to diversity and committed to plural views. Thus, no longer can European studies of Africa parade as African studies; the overthrow of the dominating canon has already begun.

A person who studies the economics of Tanzania in an economic department and then completes a dissertation on some aspect of the Tanzanian economy cannot automatically be considered an Africanist. In fact, such a person is essentially an economist albeit an economist who employs the assumptions, predispositions and methods of economics to the Tanzanian economic sector. Application of the protocols of the economic discipline to an African nation is a matter of selection not of philosophical outlook, it is a matter of temperament not of methodological discipline, a matter of fancy not of perspective.

What is difficult for some people in the field to understand is that African American Studies is not merely a collection of courses on a particular subject matter differentiated from other courses because of its emphasis on African phenomena.[3] By virtue of the work in the field it has become a method of human studies, equal to any other method of human studies in the prosecution of its work. African American Studies is a human science, that is, it is committed to discovering in human experiences, historical and contemporary, all the ways African people have tried to make their physical, social, and cultural environments serve the end of harmony. Unlike most social sciences it does not examine from a distance in order to predict behavior. Unlike some other disciplines it is neither purely social science nor humanities but a merging of the two fields as well as the use of several approaches to phenomena stemming from the Afrocentric perspective. While it is possible for the sociologist and the anthropologist to say that their fields contain nothing new, that is, nothing that is not treated in other extant sciences; the Africalogist knows that the results of the Afrocentric perspective is so profoundly revolutionary in the field of knowledge that it virtually constitutes new knowledge.

The Principal Issues in Afrocentric Inquiry

The Afrocentric enterprise is framed by cosmological, epistemological, axiological, and aesthetic issues. In this regard the Afrocentric method pursues a world voice distinctly African-centered in relationship to external phenomena. How do we gather meaning out of African or other existence?

Although I recognize the transitional nature of all cultural manifestations of a social, economic or political dimension, I also know that in the United States and other parts of the African world, culturally speaking, there is movement toward new, more cosmocultural forms of understanding. Nevertheless, meaning in the contemporary context must be derived from the most centered aspects of the African's being. When this is not the case, psychological dislocation creates automatons who are unable to fully capture the historical moment because they are living on someone else's terms. We are either existing on our own terms or the terms of others. Where will the African person find emotional and cultural satisfaction, if not in her own terms? By "term" I mean position, place or space.

Cosmological Issue

The place of African culture in the myths, legends, literatures and oratures of African people constitutes, at the mythological level, the cosmological issue within the Afrocentric enterprise. What role does the African culture play in the African's interface with the cosmos? Are dramas of life and death in this tradition reflected in metaphysical ways? How are they translated by lunar, solar, or stellar metaphors? The fundamental assumptions of Africalogical inquiry are based on the African orientation to the cosmos. By "African" I mean clearly a "composite African" not a specific discrete African orientation which would rather mean ethnic identification, i.e., Yoruba, Zulu, Nuba, etc.

There are several concerns which might be considered cosmological in the sense that they are fundamental to any research initiative in this field.

Racial Formation. Race as a social factor remains prevalent in heterogeneous but hegemonically Eurocentric societies. In the United States, the most developed example of such a society, the question of race is the most dominant aspect of intersocial relations.

Culture. A useful way to view the cultural question Afrocentrically lies in the understanding of culture as shared perceptions, attitudes, and predisposition that allow people to organize experiences in certain ways. A student of African American culture, for example, must be prepared to deal with the complex issue of "bleeding cultures," that is, the fact that African Americans constitute the most heterogeneous group in the United States biologically but perhaps one of the most homogeneous socially. Overlaps in social and cultural definitions, explanations, and solutions have to be carefully sorted out for the Africalogist to be able to determine how issues, areas, and people are joined, or differentiated in given settings. For example, something might be the result of social behaviors rather than cultural behaviors. Furthermore, the cultural behaviors may result from African American patterns from the South or from Jamaica.

Gender. Africalogy recognizes gender as a substantial research issue in questions dealing with social, political, economic, cultural, or aesthetic problems. Since the liberation of women is not an act of charity but a fundamental part of the Afrocentric project, the researcher must be cognizant of sexist language, terminology, and perspectives. It is impossible for a scholar to deal effectively with either the cultural/aesthetic or the social/behavioral concentrations without attention to the historic impact and achievement of women within the African community. Both female and male scholars must properly examine the roles women have played in liberating Africans and others from oppression, resisting the imposition of sexist repression and subjugation, and exercising economic and political authority.

Class. Class distinctions for the Afrocentrist consist in four aspects of property relations: (1) those who possess income producing properties, (2) those who possess some property that produces income and a job that supplements income, (3) those who maintain professions or positions because of skills, and (4) those who do not have skills and whose services may or may not be employed.[4]

Epistemological Issue

What constitutes the quest for truth in the Afrocentric enterprise? In Africalogy, language, myth, ancestral memory, dance-music-art, and science provide the sources of knowledge, the canons of proof and the structures of truth.

Language. Language exists when a community of people use a set of agreed upon symbols to express concepts, ideas, and psychological needs. The Afrocentric scholar finds the source of a people's truth close to the language. In the United States Ebonics serves as the archetype of African-American language.

Myth. There is an idea of preconcept, prebelief based upon the particularity of the African experience in the world. I postulate that myth, especially the central myth of the next millenium in heterogeneous but hegemonically Eurocentric societies, will be the resolution of ethnic conflict. All behavior will be rooted in experiential patterns played out in the intervention of ideas and feelings in the imposing movement of the European worldview. As Armstrong has said of the mythoform it "is strong, viable, subtle, inescapable, pervasive—operating behind each possibility of man's relationship with the world, refracting through each sense and each faculty into terms appropriate to them."[5]

Dance-Music-Art. Performing and representational art forms are central to any Afrocentric interpretation of cultural or social reality. Indeed, the fact that dance is a way of life in traditional African life and not a leisure activity to be done when one is finished with "real work" as in the West informs any Afrocentric analysis. In the diaspora the ubiquity of the dance finds its expression in the Africanization of the walkman and radio. Dance and music must be interwoven with life.

Axiological Issue

The question of value is at the core of the Afrocentric quest for truth because the ethical issues have always been connected to the advancement of African knowledge which is essentially functional.

Good. What constitutes good is a matter of the historical conditions and cultural developments of a particular society. A common expression among African Americans relates the good to the beautiful, "beauty is as beauty does" or "she's beautiful because she's good." The first statement places the emphasis on what a person does, that is, how a person "walks" among others in the society. The second statement identifies the beautiful by action. If a person's actions are not good, it does not matter how the person looks physically. Doing good is equivalent to being beautiful.

Right Conduct, therefore, represents a category of the axiological issue in Afrocentric analysis. The Afrocentric method isolates conduct rather than physical attributes of a person in literary or social analysis.

Aesthetic Issue

According to Welsh-Asante (1985), the African aesthetic is comprised of seven aspects which she calls "senses." These senses are: (1) polyrhythm, (2) polycentrism, (3) dimensional, (4) repetition, (5) curvilinear, (6) epic memory, (7) wholism.[6]

These aesthetic "senses" are said to exist as the leading elements of the African's response to art, plastic or performing. Polyrhythm refers to the simultaneous occurrence of several major rhythms. Polycentrism suggests the presence of several colors in a painting or several movements on a dancer's body occurring in the context of a presentation of art. Dimensional is spatial relationships and shows depth and energy, the awareness of vital force. Repetition is the recurring theme in a presentation of art. The recurrence is not necessarily an exact one but the theme or concept is presented as central to the work of art. Curvilinear means that the lines are curved in the art, dance, music, or poetry—this is normally called indirection in the spoken or written art forms. Epic memory carries with it the idea that the art contains the historic memory that allows the artist and audience to participate in the same celebration or pathos. Wholism is the unity of the collective parts of the art work despite the various unique aspects of the art.

The Shape of the Discipline

Centrism, the groundedness of observation and behavior in one's own historical experiences, shapes the concepts, paradigms, theories, and methods of Africalogy. In this way Africalogy secures its place alongside other centric pluralisms without hierarchy and without seeking hegemony. As a discipline, Africalogy is sustained by a commitment to centering the study of African phenomena and events in the particular cultural voice of the composite African people. Furthermore, it opens the door for interpretations of reality based in evidence and data secured by reference to the African world voice.

The anteriority of the classical African civilizations must be entertained in any Africalogical inquiry. Classical references are necessary as baseline frames for discussing the development of African cultural phenomena. Without such referent points most research would appear disconnected, without historical continuity, discrete and isolated, incidental and nonorganic.

Subject Fields

There are seven general subject fields in Africalogy: social, communication, historical, cultural, political, economic, and psychological.

A student of Africalogy chooses a research issue which falls within one or more of these subject fields. In any endeavor to uncover, analyze, criticize, or anticipate an issue, the Africalogist works to utilize appropriate methods for the subject. To examine cultural nationalism, for example, within the historical or political subject field would require a consonant method for research.

There are three paradigmatic approaches to research in Africalogy: functional, categoral, and etymological. The functional paradigm represents needs, policy, and action. In the categoral paradigm are issues of schemes, gender, class, themes, and files. The etymological paradigm deals with language, particularly in terms of word and concept origin. Studies of either sort might be conducted in the social context of African people, libraries and archives, or laboratories. The aim is to provide research that is ultimately verifiable in human experience, the final empirical authority.

A student of Africalogy might choose to perform a study in the general field of history but utilizing the functional paradigm. Or one might choose the general field of psychology and the etymological paradigm. Or one might study a topic in the general field of culture and use the categoral paradigm. Of course, other combinations are possible and the student is limited only by her or his ability to properly conceptualize the topic for study in an Afrocentric manner. Since Africalogy is not history, political science, sociology, the student must be well-grounded in the assumptions of the Afrocentric approach to human knowledge.

Scholars in our field have often been handicapped in their quest for clear and authoritative statements by a lack of methodological direction for collecting and analyzing data, choosing and interpreting research themes, approaching and appreciating cultural artifacts, and isolating and evaluating facts. As an increasingly self-conscious field African American studies has begun to produce a variety of philosophical approaches to the Afrocentric inquiry. These studies have served to underscore the need for solid methodological studies at the level of basic premises of the field and have become, in effect, pioneer works in a new perspective on phenomena.[7]

The Afrocentric psychologists have led in the reconceptualization of the field of African personality theories. Among the leaders of this field have been Wade Nobles, Joseph Baldwin, Na'im Akbar, Daudi Azibo, Linda James Myers and others. Initially calling themselves "Africentric" scholars, these intellectuals trained in psychology have explored every area of human psychology which impinges on the African experience.

Political scientists qua political scientists such as James Turner, Ronald Walters, Manning Marable, and Leonard Jeffries have argued positions that may be called Afrocentric. Only Karenga and Carruthers, however, have transformed political science and themselves and now see themselves as Afrocentrists.

The field of sociology has remained mired in a "social problem" paradigm that does not permit a fair interpretation of African data. From the days of E. Franklin Frazier, the greatest of the sociologists, the field has exhibited a double consciousness. What does a sociologist do when there are no deviant classes or societies? In the case of most African scholars in these fields, little knowledge of African Americans or Africans is available. They neither appreciate nor understand the significance of the Nile Valley or the historical response to European aggression for five hundred years.

I have consistently argued that the African American Studies or African studies scholar whom I shall call "Africalogist" must begin analysis from the primacy of the classical African civilizations, namely Kemet (Egypt), Nubia, Axum, and Meroe. This simply means that adequate understanding of African phenomena cannot occur without a reference point in the classic and most documented African culture. This is not to say that everything one writes must be shown to be tied to Egypt but it means that one cannot write fully without a self-conscious attempt to place the historical enterprise in an organic relationship to African history.

Africalogy is defined, therefore, as the Afrocentric study of phenomena, events, ideas, and personalities related to Africa.[8] The mere study of phenomena of Africa is not Africalogy but some other intellectual enterprise. The scholar who generates research questions based on the centrality of Africa is engaged in a very different research inquiry than the one who imposes Western criteria on the phenomena.

The uses of African origins of civilization and the Kemetic high culture as a classical starting point are the practical manifestations of the ways the scholar secures centrism when studying Africa. Africalogy uses the classical starting place as the beginning of knowledge. This is why Afrocentric is perhaps the most important word in the above definition of Africalogy. Otherwise one could easily think that any study of African phenomena or people constitutes Africalogy.

The geographical scope of the African world, and hence, the Africalogical enterprise, includes Africa, the Americas, the Caribbean, various regions of Asia and the Pacific. Wherever people declare themselves as African, despite the distance from the continent or the recentness of their out-migration, they are accepted as part of the African world. Thus, the indigenous people of Australia and New Guinea are considered African and in a larger context subjects for Africalogists who maintain a full analytical and theoretical discussion of African phenomena.

Although the major regions of the African culture are Africa, the Caribbean and the Americas, even within those regions there are varying degrees of cultural and technological affinity to an African world voice. Africalogy is concerned with Africans in any particular region as well as all regions. Thus, Nascimento can remind us that Brazil specifically, and South America generally, have provided an enormous amount of cultural, historical, and social data about Africans.[9] In Brazil, Zumbi, the greatest of the kings of the Republic of Palmares, Luisa Mahin and Luiz Gama are principal figures in the making of African American history; in the Dominican Republic, Diego de Campo and Lemba provide cause for celebration; in Venezuela, Oyocta, King Miguel, and King Bayano stand astride the political and social history of the region; in Columbia, there is Benkos Bioho; and in Mexico, no fighter for freedom was ever any more courageous than Yanga.

Africalogy rejects the Africanist idea of the separation of African people as being short-sighted, analytically vapid, and philosophically unsound. One cannot study Africans in the United States or Brazil or Jamaica without some appreciation for the historical and cultural significance of Africa as source and origin. A reactionary posture which claims Africalogy as "African Slave Studies" is rejected outright because it disconnects the African in America from thousands of years of history and tradition. Thus, if one concentrates on studying Africans in the inner cities of the Northeast United States, which is reasonable, it must be done with the idea in the back of the mind that one is studying African people, not "made-in-America Negroes" without historical depth.

In addition to the problem of geographical scope is the problem of gathering data about African people from oral, written and artifactal records. The work of scholars will be greatly enhanced by oral and video records that have become essential tools of analysis for contemporary African American studies. On the other hand, studies in ancient African present different challenges.

Much of the data used in a reconstructive Egyptian primacy must be artifactal since written records are barely 6,000 years old. Although humans seemed to have appeared more than 2 million years ago, the fact that permanent records are fairly new is a limiting factor in assessing with complete certainty what their existence was like during the early period.

The records are abundant enough in certain concrete areas, however, for the scholar to examine the origins of African civilizations as never before. Of course, Afrocentric approaches to these records, written or material, must be advanced. For example, because written documents are not found in a certain area does not mean that written documents did not exist. In fact, the materials upon which writing was done may not have survived. Neither can we say that in societies of priestly writing where a limited number of scribes had the knowledge of text that writing was unknown. It may have been generally not practiced while remaining specifically the function of a small cadre of scribes. Nor is it possible to make any assessment of the origin of writing with any certainty. Speculative answers are heuristic but not definitive. Thus in any discussion of the nature of records in Africa or among African people we must redefine the approach, perhaps to see writing as a stage in human history much like the introduction of radio or television.

Authors tend to write about what is accessible whether they are novelists or scholars. Therefore Christian Thomsen's 1836 interpretation of societies moving from stone to bronze to iron age was applicable to Denmark, the model for its development, and not to Japan. Definitions become contextual and experiential in terms of what the scholar knows; the more appreciation one has of other societies the less provincial the definitions should be. Of course, this does not always hold true, as it should.

We now know, of course, that these contextualized definitions are often the results of ignorance. At one time the Europeans held that the earth evolved through a series of catastrophes and that human beings emerged after the last general catastrophe. Without an appreciation for depth in time of the human race, all material remains were generally looked upon as the results of people the Europeans knew like Vikings and Phoenicians. Scholars are still trying to sort out the contributions of these seafaring people. Since the seafaring Europeans of the eighteenth and nineteenth centuries spent considerable time writing about the Vikings and Phoenicians they attributed to these people a wider array of material culture than was justified. Since we now know, however, of material artifacts that extend far beyond the 6,000-year history of the earth the European biblicalists accepted as fact we are in a better position to assess the antiquity of African civilizations.

Tournal is credited with using the term *prehistorique* in 1833 as an adjective but it was not until 1851 when Daniel Wilson wrote *The Archaeology and Prehistoric Annals of Scotland* that the idea of a discipline emerged.[10] In fact, the idea behind prehistory seems to be when written records cease to be available as you go back in time you have prehistory. Because Eurocentric writers often used race as a primary concept in discussing civilizations and cultures we are frequently called upon to "make sense" out of statements of value identified with race theory.

Any Afrocentric methodology must explain racial characteristics in a realistic manner. To begin with we must admit the strategic ambiguity of this term as it is often used. For us, race refers to the progeny of a fairly stable common gene pool which produces people with similar physical characteristics. Of course, by this definition we can quickly see that the defined gene pool may be large or small thus giving the possibility of many races. For our purposes, however, we speak of the African race meaning the gene pool defined by the whole of the African continent including people in every geographical area of the land from Egypt to South Africa, from Senegal to Kenya. The oceans constitute the biggest barriers to gene pool overflow, with the Mediterranean and Red Seas being relatively minor barriers. Although it is possible to have gene pool overflow in any direction it is most likely that the major oceans serve as fairly tight boundaries.

The Sahara is not and has never been the barrier to commerce trade or interaction among African people it has appeared to be to some writers. In fact, it is a culturally interactive arena itself and has been a greater context for such interaction in the past. Herodotus spoke of the Garamantes, whose capital now appears to have been Garama in the Libyan desert as being a people who controlled areas of the vast desert.[11] But long before the Garamantes, indeed at least 10,000 years earlier, Africans whose physical features were like those of the Hausa and Yoruba built canals and villages in the desert. Thus, we cannot speak correctly of Africa north of the Sahara or south of the Sahara; the Sahara is Africa and numerous people inhabit the Sahara.

The African race stems from a continental African gene pool and includes all of those whose ancestors originated there and who possess linguistic or cultural qualities and traits associated with the gene pool. Like other definitions of gene pools this one is imprecise. We know, for example, that in one biological sense all humans are Africans since we all possess the mitochondrial DNA of an African woman who lived about 200,000 years ago.[12] In the present historical epoch, however, African has come to mean one who has physical and cultural characteristics similar to those presently found in some region of the continent.

The definition of society useful to our discussion is an interrelated set of habits created and maintained by humans interacting. As a point of reference culture is a cognitive concept about how humans interact, create, maintain, and develop institutions inasmuch as culture exists in the brain as well as in the execution.

Although Christian Thomsen had divided prehistory into stone, bronze, and iron ages we now know that this division was too arbitrary. Societies did not all go through the same stages and if they did they went through them differentially. Furthermore, the great variety of human societies require more flexible conceptual approaches for analysis. The imposition of concepts derived from European analysis alone tends to obscure the fact that all societies have been more or less successful.

Classificatory Aspects of Africalogy

Among Africalogists the study of African phenomena is primarily an examination of cultural/aesthetic, social/behavioral, and policy issues. It is generally accepted that these three knowledge areas, judiciously studied, can be used to examine all phenomena. A growing literature in the field suggests that serious scholarship in economics or drama, history or politics, can be classified in one of the knowledge areas. Literatures are emerging around each of these cluster areas with direct interest to Africalogical issues.

Cultural/Aesthetic

By the cluster term cultural/aesthetic is meant the creative, artistic, and inventive aspect of human phenomena which demonstrates the expression of values, arts, and the good. The beautiful is a sub-category of the good and is therefore not highlighted in this definition. To be good is to be beautiful according to an Afrocentric perspective.

We reserve the term cultural/aesthetic for most of what is usually called in the West the arts and humanities: music, dance, literature, history, philosophy, painting, theater. What we study in this area are the significant elements in African phenomena, whether continental or diasporan, that give meaning to cultural character. By cultural character is meant the essence of a people's history and icons in harmonious tension. Karenga has suggested seven constituents of culture: history, religion, motif, ethos, economic, political, and social organization.[13] History is the coherent record of the achievements of a people. Religion or mythology is the ritualized manner in which a people present themselves to humanity. Motif represents the icons and symbols through which a people announce themselves. Ethos is how you are projected to the world. Economic, political, and social organizations give legitimacy and power. Karenga found these concepts to be central to any discussion of culture.

On the other hand, Diop has advanced a conception of culture which includes three factors: psychic, historic, and linguistic. In his view as seen in the *Cultural Unity of Black Africa*, the psychic factor is a mental factor; the historic deals with phenomena; and the linguistic is concerned with languages.[14] Diop's intention is to demonstrate the unity of African culture by examining these factors.

In order to capture Karenga's constituents while not losing sight of Diop's traditional factors I have integrated these most prominent conceptualizations into a cultural framework with three key elements:

Epistemic:	ethics, politics, psychology (modes of behavior)
Scientific:	history, linguistics, economics (methods of investigation)
Artistic:	icons, art, motifs, symbols (types of presentation)

Although I recognize the overlapping potential of certain areas I am convinced that such a classification as has been made here is valuable for understanding areas of inquiry on the cultural question.

Many important ideas and innovations, particularly in the artistic sphere, have gone either unrecognized or been badly misunderstood because of a lack of Afrocentric methodology. There is no way to properly appreciate the Rap, or break dancing, for example, without a cultural/aesthetic perspective in African and African American cultural history. A child does not give birth to itself.

Some Afrocentrists like Rosalind Jeffries tie most cultural and artistic expressions of the African world to the Nile Valley civilizations or show the possibility of the diffusion of the ideas over a great period of time through transformation into the present era.[15] Niangoran-Bouah has done similar work with the gold-weights of Ghana; Diop showed the interconnectedness of the graphic systems of West African nations with ancient Kemet, Welsh-Asante has developed the *umfundalai* technique of dance essentially around the primacy of the Nile Valley civilizations, and Meyerwitz has shown the continuation of the Egyptian kingship system in the Ghanaian kingship system.[16] This field of cultural science is relatively new in the way it is being articulated and will make a major contribution to reinterpretation of African cultural/aesthetic phenomena.

Social/Behavioral

The social/behavioral cluster refers to the area of knowledge that deals with human behavior in relationship to other humans, living or dead, relationship to the cosmos, and relationship to self. It is the area normally covered in the American system by fields such as sociology, psychology, economics, political science, urban studies, religion, and anthropology among other fields. As it is expressed in our discussion of phenomena the social/behavioral cluster includes the critique of Eurocentric interpretations of African phenomena as well. Therefore, it is both an analysis and a criticism of the manner African social or behavioral data have been interpreted.

The criticism derives from the need to set the record straight. Indeed the idea found embedded in European thought, particularly in the seventeenth, eighteenth, nineteenth, and twentieth centuries that Africans were inferior socially and behaviorally has tainted most of what passes for social science in the West, definitionally and conceptually. Few have been able to escape Alexander Pope's dictum in the *Essay on Man* (1733) "some are, and must be, greater than the rest" and its implication for European contact and interpretation of that contact with the rest of the world.[17]

Stephen Jay Gould argues in *The Mismeasure of Man* that biological determinism, the idea that those perceived to be on the bottom, are made of poor brains or bad genes, was a shared context of European and American thinking about racial ranking.[18] In fact, Gould contends that while racial prejudice may be as old as recorded history, "its biological justification imposed the additional burden of intrinsic inferiority upon despised groups, and precluded redemption by conversion or assimilation."[19]

The publication of Charles Darwin's *The Origin of the Species* in 1859 and his subsequent thirteen years of publications devoted to expanding and applying his notion of natural selection, which James Chesebro has shown persuasively is an oxymoron, the combining of two contradictory terms without reducing the tension between them to form a new concept, created an intellectual climate for all kinds of racist and sexist notions about human achievement, reproduction, and worth.[20] Indeed, Darwin worked within the general anti-African canon while at the same time attempting to state a theory of evolution which was against the intellectual wisdom of the day. Thus, social and racial motivations operated in Darwin's work as a function of the European male's presentation of self as the highest human form. Of course this is a self-serving formulation for the definer. The argument is generally stated in this fashion: when individuals compete for scarce resources to survive and reproduce, those who are more successful at securing a greater proportion of the resources generate more offspring and consequently their kind is reproduced at a greater rate of increase because the fittest has survived. All of this is based upon the idea that the ratio of reproductive increase is so great that it leads to struggle. However, human population may recommend some other, more humane view, of the evolutionary process.

From such damaged intellectual ideas as biological determinism came Social Darwinism, Kindly Paternalism, and a myriad of white justifications for the imposition of Eurocentrism as universal. As Michael Bradley says in *Iceman Inheritance*, the European was more aggressive than others due to, he believed, the nature of the historical evolution in Europe itself.[21] Nevertheless, the ideas of these writers have colored the minds of some of the most influential social scientists in Europe and America. A strong list could be made of the early progenitors of racial thinking: H. J. Eysenck, Louis Bolk, Cesare Lombroso, Paul Broca, Robert M. Yerkes, C. C. Brigham, Robert Bean, G. Stanley Hall, Charles Spearman. One can certainly find individuals such as these for any field of endeavor who contributed to the racist social/behavioral context making it necessary for reevaluative analysis and critique.

Policy Issues

Africalogy is necessarily an area which encompasses all political, social, and economic issues confronting the African world. The policy issue cluster includes discussion and debate around what should or ought to be political, social, cultural, or economic actions in response to critical conditions affecting African communities. Some of the policy issues involved in this field of study are health, education, welfare, and employment. Each of these issues may be researched, discussed, and resolved within the framework of an Afrocentric analysis. For example, an inquiry into health problems within the African-American community must begin with an understanding of the role played by communal beliefs in various ways—e.g., how to eradicate disease, how to mask and minimize pain, how to secure the most effective health delivery to an African-American community bent on having a hoodoo priest present whenever a medical doctor enters a case.

The Problems of Method

All methods of doing research have philosophical roots with specific assumptions about phenomena, human inquiry, and knowledge. The Africanist's frame of reference has too often been Eurocentric, that is, flowing from a conceptualization of African people developed to support the Western version of Africa. The problem exists because so much of the Western tradition is firmly grounded in Hegel's conception of history. Hegel elaborated three histories or three ways of writing history: original, reflective, and philosophical.[22] Original history, such as that of Herodotus and Thucydides, describes actions, events, and conditions which the historian saw with his own eyes or received reports of from others.

These primary historians are concerned with "what is actual and living in their environment."[23] Such a history is a contemporary report of events and conditions. In Hegel's sense of original history certain sociologists or anthropologists might be said to be historians.

Reflective history may be universal, pragmatic, critical, or fragmentary. In its so-called "universal" form it seeks to survey an entire people, country, or the world. Hegel sees problems with this method of history, chief of which is the remarkable ability of some historians to not transfer their contemporary frame of mind to the period they are writing about at the moment. Thus, he describes a Livian history that makes Roman kings and generals speak in the manner of lawyers of the Livian era and not in the traditions of Roman antiquity.

The pragmatic form allows the historian to write about past events at a present time; the confluence of events and conditions, assist in nullifying the past, and therefore all periods of history, in spite of themselves, must decide within and in accordance with its own age. Fascinated by the idea of spirit, Hegel does not count reflective history valuable unless it is history committed to exploring the deep patterns of a people. Hegel's condemnation of German reflective histories is not that they did not follow the French example of creating a present for themselves and referring the past to the present condition.

Critical history is the "evaluation of historical narratives and examination of their truth and trustworthiness."[24] The key contribution of this method is in the ability of the author to extract results from narration rather than events. Although Hegel is content to isolate this form as a part of the reflective method of history he is critical of it as history. Historiography, for example, could not rightly be called history and higher criticism was itself suspect because of what Hegel sees as its "subjective fancies" replacing definite facts.

The fourth form of reflective history is fragmentary. Hegel writes that it is "abstractive but, in adopting universal points of view for example the history of art, of law, of religion—it forms a transition to philosophical world history."[25] The aim of this kind of conceptual history is always to find the guide to the inner soul of a people. Hegel's metaphysics, the principal introduction of metaphysics for the Western world, comes out in his notions of guides of the soul, the idea is in truth, the spirit, rational and necessary will. It is impossible to understand Hegel's concept of reflective history without knowing that for him history is really spirit performing in time as nature is idea in space.[26]

The third Hegelian method of history is philosophical. He finds the need to justify this type of historical method because unlike the cases of the original and reflective histories the concept is not self-explanatory. The Hegelian concept of philosophical history is the thoughtful contemplation of history on the basis of data of reality. This he contrasts to philosophy which allegedly produces its own ideas out of speculation, without regard to given data.

Critics may assume that "objectivity" is compromised when the investigator uses the descriptive mode for Afrocentric research. The Afrocentricist does not accept the European concept of objectivity because it is invalid operationally. Dona Richards is correct to evaluate the concept of "objectivity" negatively in her brilliant essay.[27] I have argued that what often passes for objectivity is a sort of collective European subjectivity. Therefore, it may not serve any useful purpose to speak of objectivity and subjectivity as this division is artificial in and of itself. The Afrocentricist speaks of research that is ultimately verifiable in the experiences of human beings, the final empirical authority. Of course, the methods of proof are founded upon the principles of fairness and openness. Both concepts are based in the idea of doing something that can be shown to be fair in its procedure and open in its application. What is unconscionable is the idea that when a person makes any decision that the decision is "objective"; every decision, even one's choice of software for her or his word processor, is human and consequently "subjective."

One cannot conduct an authentic debate on the political philosophies of Jefferson, Hume, or Locke without a discussion of their doctrines of racial supremacy, sexism, exploitation of other nationalities, colonialism and slavery. The true scholar must seek to assess the views of the political theorists in light of the cultural, racial class, and gender context. The point is, no field of human knowledge can be divorced from its author's involvement as a human being in a given context.

Some critics assume that the investigator may rely too much on his or her own opinions in collecting data from a social context with which the investigator is familiar. The Afrocentric method proposes the dual-collection paradigm to deal with that problem particularly as it relates to what may be cross-cultural or cross-national research projects. This is important because in too many cases the Eurocentric method allows an individual researcher to conduct research on his or her own. In many cases in Africa, graduate students from American and European universities conduct research in communities that they have little in common with and expect to be able to make sense out of without assistance. This is probably one of the biggest sins of the Eurocentric methods. These students assume they can insure "objectivity" and make some sense out of what they discover in African communities. If accurate results are obtained it is often by default and luck not because of some "objective" method.

Two directives are invoked whenever the Africalogical research-er seeks to make a cross-cultural or trans-racial study. (1) The use of two researchers to collect similar data, at least one of whom must be from the social or cultural context, and (2) the assessment of the data by two evaluators, at least one of whom must be from the social or cultural context. In addition to the use of the dual-collection model researchers using the descriptive approach will also employ triangulation of information and in-depth interviews.

The nomothetic model of experimental laboratory research insists that variable control and manipulation are able to assist in universal laws is highly questionable. "Universal" is again one of those Eurocentric terms that has little meaning in the real world. People live in societies and operate within cultures. The aim of the descriptive researcher has to be the in-depth knowledge of a social/human context in order to be able to make some sense out of it, to appreciate it, to live in peace with it. In actuality, this is counter to the experimental framework that is based on the logic of prediction, war, and the market. What is the need for the universal idea, the control and manipulation of variables, the predictive ability of the researchers? Based on the war games model, the Eurocentric social scientists went to the boards and to computers to be able to predict human behavior under adverse circumstances. This model has now been used in market research, particularly by advertising interests, in order to sell more products to African and Asian nations. The Afrocentric method must have a different goal; it must find its reason to be in the harmonizing mission. This is an interactive model rather than a distant, sterile, abstract, isolated, and non-contact model. Rather this method finds its strength in the cooperative and integrative function of human experiences.

Edmund Husserl's *Ideas: General Introduction to Phenomenology* provoked discussion around the issue of methodology in European social sciences.[28] Husserl's introduction of phenomenology was a major advance for the social sciences. In fact, taking many of his ideas from continental African philosophy, Husserl posited a wholistic view rather than a detached, isolated, disparate, reality. The phenomenologist's search for essence by questioning all assumptions about reality is similar to the Afrocentricist's search for essence by questioning all assumptions about reality that are rooted in a particularistic view of the universe.

The distortion of social reality by traditional Eurocentric scientific methods occurs because of allegiance to a set of false propositions. One such proposition appears in the formulation where the researcher is separate from the object of study and in fact seeks to gain as much distance as possible from the object. Both the phenomenologists and the Afrocentricists reject the separation of investigator/subject relationship though for different reasons. The Afrocentricist finds the wholistic impulse naturally from the cultural environment. Whether one talks of reality in the African American church or in African dance one sees that separation of subject/object, speaker/audience, dancer/spectators or investigator/subject is artificial. The social context of African people encourages a collective as opposed to an individual separation.

The Afrocentric method insists that the researcher examines herself or himself in the process of examining any subject. Thus, the process of examination involves introspection and retrospection. Introspection means that the researcher questions herself or himself in regards to the topic under discussion. One might write down all one believes and thinks about a topic prior to beginning the research project. The reason for this is to ascertain what obstacles exist to an Afrocentric method in the researcher's own mind. Retrospection is the process of questioning one's self after the project has been completed to ascertain if any personal obstacles exist to a fair interpretation.

The hypothetical-statistical model found in modern Eurocentric methods is interventionist in the research project because it forces the researcher's biases on both inquiry and analysis. Afrocentric method suggests cultural and social immersion as opposed to "scientific distance" as the best approach to understand African phenomena. This process in itself is extremely difficult because it means that the researcher must have some familiarity with the history, language, philosophy, and myths of the people under study. It goes without saying that other methods often assume that the researcher need not know anything about the culture in order to undertake a project. Furthermore, without cultural immersion the researcher loses all sense of ethical value and becomes a researcher "for the sake of research," the worse kind of value in the Afrocentric approach which sees research as assisting in the humanizing of the world. In a European world one can have intercultural communicationists doing intercultural research who do not believe in intercultural communication, except as a way to sell market products, attitudes, or beliefs.

The Afrocentric method shares some of the perceptions of the so-called "ethnomethodology" but differs in both its philosophical base and its conceptualization. What it shares with ethno-methodology is the idea that reality is a process and that the discussion of normative patterns cannot be made intelligently unless the researcher understands the social context. What I have difficulty with is the Eurocentric foundation of Harold Garfinkel's view.[29] Although Garfinkel argued correctly that researchers should not assume common meaning is shared, he incorrectly assumed that the structure that accounted for subjects' perceptions was above and beyond the contextual meaning of their particular culture.

But the principal problem with ethnomethodology is its Euro-centric bias. What is ethnomethodology conceptually but the white Western Eurocentric researcher saying to other white Western Eurocentric researchers that "we ought to study these other people from their own contexts"? "Ethno" is derived from "ethnic" which is derived from the medieval English "ethnik" and the late Latin "ethica" which means "heathen." Since the Eurocentric writers did not initially include white people in their conceptualization one can only speculate that ethnomethodology, like ethnomusicology, was meant to study those who were not Europeans.

Our methodology must be wholistic and integrative; our epistemology, participatory and committed. The Africalogist is a working scholar committed to the advancement of knowledge about the African world. In pursuing a vision in Afrocentric scholarship the Africalogist gathers facts about African phenomena, verifies them and subjects the interpretations to the strictest measures. The aim of the Africalogist is to make the world more meaningful to those who live in it and to create spaces for human understanding. Our task is not like that of the Western social scientist who seeks to predict human behavior in order to advance more direct control over nature but rather to explain human nature as it is manifest in the African arena. All statements about objects, phenomena, and events are subjects for discussion, analysis, and action. To be a good Africalogist, the scholar must be able to distinguish between Afrocentric statements and less precise non-Afrocentric statements.

The following statements, with their obvious biases, are found in contemporary Eurocentric scholarly works:

> ... the Apollo embodies a higher state of civilization than the mask. They both represent spirits, messengers from another world. ... To the negro imagination it is a world of fear and darkness, ready to inflict horrible punishment for the smallest infringement of a taboo to the Hellenistic imagination it is a world of light and confidence in which gods are like ourselves, only more beautiful, and descend to earth in order to teach men reason and the laws of harmony.[30]

> They were forced to subjugate numbers of still primitive peoples as well as more civilized states. Two empires, both of which had reached a fairly high level of civilization, disappeared when the Spaniards arrived; the empire of the Aztecs in Mexico and that of the Incas in Peru.[31]

In these two typical statements by Eurocentric writers one senses the bias against other cultures. Clarke, well-respected as a major force in European culture, demonstrates his prejudice against African culture and his ignorance of African art. He chooses to compare the Apollo with the mask, any mask, rather than to compare the Apollo with the Ramses at Abu Simbel or some similar sculpture from African classical antiquity. His contrast of a world of fear and a world of confidence represents self-conscious attempts to valorize the European experience above the African. The fact is that anyone capable of manipulating language could play the same game. One surely would not compare Stonehenge with the Pyramids. Rodrigues places his prejudices not so much in comparisons as in omissions which, if they had been stated, would show Spanish destruction of other civilizations. For example, he says the Spaniards "were forced to subjugate" as if some divine force caused them to attack the people of the country. Furthermore, the indigenous civilizations are said to have "disappeared" when the Spaniards arrived. This type of research writing has soured the whole process of the search for truth. Our methods must be devoid of obvious prejudices.

The key factor in the articulation of method in the non-Afrocentric social sciences and humanities is the subservience to method. A defining characteristic becomes the absolute necessity to submit to method. Thus rather than method growing out of human contact with situation it is imposed and in this imposition dominates the scholar's work. A correspondence of this is found in society at large where technical administration is assumed to be superior when it is carried out under the most severe procedures. Marcusean one-dimensionality is the assertion of technology's imperial advance in the industrialized world. When Charles Lakes, the African-American Olympian gymnast, was chosen to represent the United States in the Seoul Olympics of 1988, a coach was quoted as saying about Lakes' training style that he lacked discipline sometimes in his training. What the coach was reacting to is the same creative syncopation one finds in jazz as opposed to European concert music. What he sees as discipline is merely the attention to external procedures whereas the African often works on an internal rhythm. Lakes' result was probably as good as those who practiced a more one-dimensional linear discipline! A set linear regimen often goes against the principles of African culture. It is not a question of capability, either for the European-cultured or African-cultured person but rather how one learns to achieve. This is precisely why one can argue that power, immanent energy, force, vitality, are all expressions of the dynamism which resides in objects and ideas for the African world culture.

Africalogy builds upon theoretical principles outlined by previous scholars. Any intelligent selection of a field of inquiry or a question for research must be based on a theory. The fundamental theoretical bases for Africalogy are derived from the Afrocentric perspective. Since the Africalogists must select from a vast galaxy of facts for a study; it is the theoretical principle which assists the Africalogist in determining the questions to ask and the methods to use in acquiring data which will answer the questions.

Using history as the fundamental integrater of data, Africalogists seek to perform three important functions:

1. Provide logical explanations of African peoples' experiences from the origin of civilization to the present.
2. Develop a wholistic approach to the role of Africa in world culture.
3. Explain the behavior of African people by interpretations and analysis derived from an Afrocentric perspective.

These functions underscore Karenga's concept of historical fundamentalism where he claims history to be the key discipline in providing a knowledge base. But Karenga's notions are much more Afrocentric, clearly more supportive of the human family, than, say, Hegel's Germanic particularity, which became for the Europeans the way to analyze history.

Although Karenga's position is correct, history is not the equivalent of Africalogy. Indeed, Hegelian oriented African American historians often assume that because they teach and write African American history that they are in African American studies. The late historian Nathan Huggins made such a faux pas with his 1986 report to the Ford Foundation. Huggins made the critical mistake of confusing programs and departments in his assessment of "African-American" studies.

The Hegelian formulation of the historical method is filled with problems for the Afrocentrists. In the first place Hegel bases his concept of history on writing. Although this is understandable within the context of his discussion of European reason as the principal mode through which western philosophy influences history it is unforgivable in light of the nature of oral logic. Indeed, even the oft-quoted Greeks understood the significance of orality both in it informative and persuasive forms. Of course the Greeks were closer to Africa than we are often led to believe.

Furthermore, the relatively offhanded dismissal of myths, folk songs and traditions as not a part of original history raises serious questions about Hegel's view of the world. He says that myths, folksongs and traditions are "obscure modes and peculiar to obscure peoples."[32] According to Hegel, these "obscure peoples" are not people who know who they are and what they want. Of course what he is really attacking is the collective nature of the mythic, or epic expression. Hegel finds a "firm individuality" as the only basis for history.

This is fundamentally unacceptable to the Africalogist. It is because of such formulations that the Livingston-Stanley duet in the African forest becomes history while hundreds of thousands of people living in the same time and space are said to be without history. An intellectual dishonesty allows history to be what happened to two Europeans in the midst of hundreds of thousands of Africans. In Hegelian terms Africans are an obscure people, obscure in this instance because Europeans do not know them but certainly not obscure to their own recorders, musicians, historians, epics, myths, and chronicles.

Hegel's position on Greece is like that of other European and American writers, indeed they view the Greek experience as a virgin birth of their own experience; of course, in numerous forms what has paraded as Greece derived is actually African derived. Hegel's predicament is even more complex because in philosophy he demonstrates an awesome ignorance of ancient African civilizations placing Egypt, even at this time, at the bottom of world civilizations. This was principally a Eurocentric reaction to an African civilization and since Hegel did have the benefit of reading the work of the French writers and scholars who wrote of the monumental nature of an African civilization, he could admit, with reluctance, the anteriority of Egypt, but he would not admit, even reluctantly, that Egypt was a high culture.

Furthermore, he is definite in his opinions about the supremacy of the Germanic people: "Only the Germanic peoples came, through Christianity, to realize that man as man is free and that freedom of Spirit is the very essence of man's nature."[33] Inherent in Hegel's view of human nature and the role of world spirit in human matters is the belief that there is always "a dominant people" in whose history is the unfolding of the dominant phase of any epoch.[34] The characteristics of Hegel's ethnocentric mind are seen in his presentation of the four historical worlds: Oriental, Greek, Roman, and German. He argues, in effect, that the rest of the world serves as an audience for the central position of each of these cultures. I am not the first to point to Hegel's arrogantly

Eurocentric view of history. Walsh has written that Hegel's point of view is "indeed aggressively European."[35]

⌈The key to an adequate analysis of Hegel's posture on history is his prosecution of an ethnocentric perspective as if it were universal. To claim, as he did, that Africa, the birthplace of the oldest human civilizations, was devoid of morality and consequently ahistorical, was to demonstrate both an aggressive Eurocentrism and an ignorance of Africa. Granted that at the time of Hegel's first lectures Europeans did not understand the full significance of the African continent in the evolution of human society and paleontology; however, the lack of humility in the face of this ignorance is without defense.⌋

To prosecute the maligning of Africa it was necessary for Hegel to advance a false division of the continent, a division superimposed on the land, not by the people of the continent themselves, but by European historians, anthropologists, and colonial administrators who said Africa consisted of Asian Africa, European Africa, and Africa proper. In *Philosophy of History* he explained that Africa proper was the territory south of the Sahara; European Africa was the territory north of the Sahara; Egypt was the part of Africa connected to Asia. This division is arbitrary and has no validity in point of fact. Africa is geographically and culturally, due to natural barriers, more continental than Europe. There is neither an Africa north of the Sahara nor south of the Sahara as Hegel claimed; the Sahara is Africa and human populations have inhabited the Sahara for thousands of years. It is as useless to speak of Africa separated by deserts as it is to speak of separations by rain forests. What Hegel and others of his school of thought have attempted to argue since the emergence of the Aryan model is that Africa in its northern areas was somehow different qualitatively from Africa in the southern areas. This is why Hegel could say of Africa that it was "a land of childhood, which lying beyond the day of self-conscious history, is enveloped in the dark mantle of night."[36] Such commentary shows an extreme disregard for the historical processes carried out by Africans in various cultural and social contexts for many millennia. Indeed, Egypt, the grandest civilization of antiquity, was necessarily seen in Hegel's view as belonging more to Arabic influences than African, despite the fact that African civilization in Egypt had flourished 4,000 years prior to the coming of the Arabs.

Hegel must have been aware of the contradictory bases of his discussion of African geography. One cannot assert the continental definition of Africa geographically while trying to deny Africa's unity culturally or historically, that is, asserting that the "real Africa" is actually only in a portion of the continent. European Africa, of course, never existed and was merely the Hegelian attempt to Germanicize all of those people who may have contributed to African coastal civilizations. Hegel's claims for northern Africa being European or Asian are no more to be accepted or believed than someone else's claims that southern Europe was actually African Europe. Cheikh Anta Diop is most authoritative on this question, contending that a black African people occupied the northern part of the African continent since "prehistoric" times.[37]

As to Egypt being connected to Asia, as Hegel claims without any evidence, Diop is most clear:

> if a civilization comparable to that of Egypt had flowered there [in Asia] ... its memory, no matter how vague, would have been transmitted to us by the Ancients, who form one branch of the Indo-Europeans, who furnished so many corroborative testimonials on the Negro-Egyptian culture.[38]

What is more certain, however, is the intimate connection of ancient Egypt with Nubia, Punt, Libya, and Ethiopia. Since the Nile River is the principal organ of Egyptian social, historical, civic and monumental life, is not it natural that the civilizations of the Nile Valley would be more closely related to ancient Egypt than more distant and less accessible lands?

Perhaps one of the most revealing statements in the *Philosophy of History* is Hegel's assurances that "among the Negroes moral sentiments are quite weak, or more strictly speaking, nonexistent."[39] Such rhetoric was probably not unusual as the spirit of the time in Europe was one of racial expansionism and growing sentiments for the doctrine of Germanic racial supremacy. Morality would prove in both the nineteenth and twentieth centuries not to be a special attribute reserved for Germanic peoples.

Hegel's place in Eurocentrism is supreme and next to Plato he is the most influential thinker in the European pantheon. But his speculative idealism in historical thinking has led to some permutations that have entrapped the best minds of Europe and America. Without a doubt Hegel's influence on sociology, history, political science, and philosophy remains prominent and insidious. Its prominence is seen in the quotations, allusions, and examples taken from his works by contemporary scholars; his insidiousness is found in the structure of thought found in the writings of European and American scholars. While it is true that Hegel's ideas on the Absolute, the world spirit, dialectics, and ethical idealism provoked some reaction in the works of the Marxists, Kierkegaard, G. E. Moore, and others, he nevertheless was seldom checked by his European critics or followers for his racist views regarding Africans. Furthermore, the works of Theodor Adorno and Herbert Marcuse, although rooted in Hegelian ideas and used for quite different purposes than Hegel may have appreciated, are valuable for their endeavor to forge new relevance out of Hegel's dialectic. Yet German writers such as Karl Löwith believes that the Hegelian philosophy was responsible for the historicist crisis which led to Marx and Kierkegaard as opposed to a Goethean serenity based on the eternal return motif. Historicism itself owes a large debt to Hegel's influence. But historicism has raised numerous questions among philosophers and the ensuing debates have thrown light on the nature of the European anxiety over method.

Karl Popper's attack on historicism, the ideology of laws of history and development, has been answered in part by the work of Michel Foucault and Thomas Kuhn in the prosecution of their view that systems of thought are essentially the products of rules.[40] Of course, these rules are often unclear to the practitioners of the systems and only become evident to those who retrospectively reflect on the meaning of social development, human nature, or social relations.

This debate deepens rather than eliminates the errors inherent in an overreaching domestic squabble within Eurocentric intellectual circles. There can be no either-or positions which are taken on every issues and in science, philosophy, history, and sociology. In one thing Popper is correct and that is the poverty of historicism which has given birth to pernicious and rigid doctrines that endanger human freedom. Beyond this, however, is the matter of strict systems of thought that engender either-or positions. The real poverty exists in the tradition that pits historicism against ahistoricism, structuralism against deconstruction, white against black, etc. These are illusions built into our response patterns by the contemporary emphasis on either-or situations.

Paul Feyerabend recognizes the illusionary status of any kind of framework and claims that anarchy must replace rationalism in the theory of knowledge.[41] His position, supported by a growing number of converts, is that intellectual progress can only be achieved by stressing creativity, wishes, and intuitions rather than the method and authority of science. While I submit that Feyerabend has advanced Western thought in regards to knowledge, one must not misunderstand the nature of his significant enterprise in a world context. The Afrocentrist has never abandoned the position that knowledge must be sought in every human encounter with self, nature and the cosmos. Thus, *Against Method* simply rejects the rationalist merry-go-round and argues for the "withering away of reason" because "the only principle which does not inhibit progress is anything goes." On one hand, the differences between Popper and Feyerabend are significant; on another, the notion of framework creates anxiety equally in both. To a large degree, their concerns have found articulation in Sartre's existentialism which sees society as absurd, cruel, and without mercy on the poor lonely individual. Feyerabend particularly rushes to disavow allegiance to any method.

To the contrary, Africalogy advances on all fronts simultaneously. It does not deny rationalism its historical place but neither does it deny other forms of human inquiry their places in the acquisition of knowledge. The human being can reason without lessons in logic and can learn without being instructed. To advance knowledge the fundamental ingredients have to be openness to all possibilities, freedom of thought, evaluation of all data received by the human person, and the integration of all methods advanced by human beings into the intellectual inquiry. Methods of history, literary criticism, history of science, botany, economics, zoology, biology, politics, medicine, and law are not necessarily contradictory and cannot be dismissed as unimportant in the search for understanding of the human condition.

They must be criticized, however, for their exclusion of the "other," for their construction of an either-or paradigm, and for their antifeminist posture. And pointedly in the context of Africalogy, most of the European-derived sciences and arts treat Africans and African contributions as irrelevant to knowledge acquisition. Such arrogance stands at the door to most fields of European studies. Any examination of religion, for example, will show that few books on religion actually give as much weight to African religions as to Judaism, Christianity, Islam, Hinduism, and Buddhism. This is the case although Africans were the first people recorded to have a concept of religion. Furthermore, at least one African religion, Yoruba, has grown into an international religion with more than 100 million adherents.

One must often use different sensibilities to gain access to knowledge; these sensibilities give Afrocentric methods greater absorption capacities. If we examine history, we must also discard some of the traditional patterns of asking questions to obtain knowledge. Thus, to determine how the hospitality shown to Europeans by members of King Anse's Fanti royal family in Ghana in 1482 was misunderstood, the scholar applies a multiplicity of methods while maintaining the essential core Afrocentric perspective.

In reality, this means looking at the encounter from the standpoint of the Fanti rather than the Portuguese—the relatively un-discussed as opposed to the more discussed—through examination of oral traditions, linguistics, material transformation, court changes in Fanti, external trade patterns as a result of the encounter, legends, myths, or any rumors found among non-Fanti peoples.

The Africalogist advances beyond the mechanistic moment and grasps the dynamic and rhythmic process by which we live-in-the-world. This living-in-the-world becomes the ground in which we find authentic empiricism. In this respect Afrocentric inquiry is both particular and general inquiry. It is particular inquiry in the sense that it engages the scholar creatively as a person who lives in the world; it is general because it operates as social inquiry encompassing psychological, cultural, and mythical dimensions of human life, thereby superseding the mechanistic model with its rather static profile.

Trained in Eurocentric perspectives most contemporary scholars have only seen from a Eurocentric viewpoint and this view is decidedly different from that of the African person who has been victimized by the imposition of Eurocentric expression. Afrocentricity is inevitably the philosophy of African scholarship in this historical moment. One cannot transcend it until it has been exhausted in its confrontation with our reality. The circumstances, the set of circumstances are uniquely social, but it is only out of the social environment that one is able to derive the authentic empirical experience, otherwise we are playing "head games."[42]

The failure of the "Africanists" to make any real gains against the dominant and dominating white and Western ethos that is at the base of so many of Africa's problems is precisely due to the predicament of contradiction. These Africanists, whether black or as is most often the case, white, are trapped in theoretical and methodological prisons from which they can only escape with great danger to their reputations. Since they are participating in a Western enterprise and seek the accoutrements that come with that enterprise they must add to the store of theory or method that builds that enterprise no matter what the area of study. Thus for the Africanist who studies the economy of Kenya, the aim is to add to economic theory and method, a Western enterprise, more than to add to the liberation of the African nation's economy from the grip of the West. The same can be said about the historian, anthropologist, linguistician; only the Afrocentric scholar rises to a new level of consciousness which claims that it is the concrete act of turning the table so that Africa assumes centrality that grants African people a new economic, historical or linguistic vision. Indeed, we make the future by virtue of realizing in our actions the predominant objective task for restructuring the present. The authentic empirical experience is living-in-the-world with an appreciation of the individual as the motive force for social reconstruction. Afrocentric method approaches all African phenomena from the standpoint of African centrality. Naturally this centrality cannot be left to chance, it must respond to a theoretical framework where each phenomenon is examined within the context of the authentic empiricism so fundamental to the methodology.

The leap of imagination one finds in the best Afrocentric scholars gets its energy from the African aesthetic sensibility. What one seeks in a study is the merger of facts with beauty; this becomes the creative quest for interpretation which "looks good" while it is explaining. Any time a scholar reaches a dead end in interpretation or analysis it is usually because he or she is utilizing the traditional methods. New discoveries will be made in authentically new ways on the edge of risk.[43] Such studies will undoubtedly receive grudging admiration at first but they represent the only exit from a Eurocentric, male dominated view of the world. We are led to the African-centered idea of wholism, everything is everything, and we are a part of the one and the other is our own measure. To begin this pilgrimage towards disentanglement will mean that we must find intellectual paths which have long been covered by the superimposition of monoethnic ideas as universal.

C. Tsehloane Keto, the brilliant Afrocentrist, has written in his provocative historiography, *The Africa Centered Perspective of History*, that "different regions of the world that have evolved distinct cultures are entitled to develop paradigms based on the perspectives of the region's qualitatively significant human cultures, histories and experiences."[44] He believes that a perspective called "pluriversal" can only occur by "extrapolating global rather than regional trends."[45] Indeed, Keto believes that "the trouble at present is that studies about the rest of the world are overly influenced and often distorted by theories and conclusions drawn from studies based on a minority of the world's families, a minority of the world's women, a minority of the world's social structures and a minority of the world's cultures."[46]

The insights of scholars such as Keto provide the basis for Africalogical theories. Here the work of Lucius Outlaw must be considered in the philosophical context of the emergence of Africalogy. In fact, in his seminal paper "Africology: Normative Theory" written in 1987, Outlaw explains the necessity of rules governing a discipline. He says that "the rules—the norms—for obtaining such agreement are not provided by melanin."[47] In this,

Outlaw underscores the position I have taken when discussing Afrocentricity. As a theory it is not, nor can it be based on biological determinism. Anyone willing to submit to the discipline of learning the concepts and methods may acquire the knowledge necessary for analysis.

In a sense, a revolution has already begun. Led by a host of Kemetic scholars of African origin and with the participation of several European scholars, the movement toward decolonizing information and approaches to information has touched ancient chronology, classificatory studies of civilization, African American literary studies, resistance activities of colonized and enslaved peoples, and the structure of knowledge itself. It is particularly important for us to advance a more reasonable chronology and real perspective of ancient Egypt.

PART II

ANTERIORS

George E. Brooks has posited a periodization of western Africa independent of European chronology.[1] This is an advance that adds to an African-centered construction of time periods. Indeed, Brooks makes his case on the basis of rainfall records in the Sahel and Sahara regions.

> For some eight millennia, from ca. 18000 until ca. 10000 B.C., while Europe and North America experienced the last period of extensive glaciation, the northern part of the African continent sustained extremely arid conditions.[2]

By using the period 1930-1960 as a base period for determining rainfall and aridity in the Sahara (during the base period the annual rainfall was approximately 100 mm), Brooks showed that between 9000-6000 B.C. there were "populations inhabiting the Sahara area and a wide belt of territory extending southwards along the upper Nile Valley and into the Lakes region of East Africa [which] shared a way of life that J. E. G. Sutton has characterized as the Aquatic Civilization of Middle Africa."[3]

Brooks' periodization attempts to use an African-centered basis for establishing the chronology of Africa. If one looks at the rise of civilization in the northeastern corner of the continent one sees that the Kemetic people's rise is nearly parallel with the time markers one finds in the western part of the continent, particularly in relationship to the trading villages along the Niger River bend. Documentation of the Niger River bend civilizations is not as extensive at the present time as that in the Nile Valley.

The Kemetic Anteriority

The first extensively documented people to occupy Kemet, the land now known as Egypt were the Badarians, a black, African people who are authoritatively dated to 6,000 B.C. Although San and Twa types are said to go back to 30,000 B.C., evidences of their presence are largely found in the desert rock paintings rather than everyday artifactual evidences such as pottery and hunting implements. On the other hand, the Badarians left a strong record of artifactual evidences and their morphological character also is well established.

The usual period classification of Kemetic history consists of two chronological phases: (1) predynastic and (2) dynastic. The predynastic phase is imprecise in its origin. I have chosen therefore to speak of the remote predynastic and the near predynastic. The remote predynastic is from the initial human occupation of Kemet to the Badarian age. The near predynastic is from the Badarian period to the uniting of the two lands by Menes the Great.

The near predynastic period can be divided into the Badarian, Amratean, and Gerzean ages. Establishing the Badarian morphological character is necessary to counter what Davidson, Bernal, and Carruthers have seen as the anti-African positions taken by European scholars during the nineteenth century.[4] European scholars, following Hegel, insisted that no civilizations were developed by Africans. Therefore, they showed antipathy to the idea that the first Egyptians were, in fact, black.

The Morphological Character

Most previous work examining the morphology of the Badarians, even when attempting to present a constructive thesis, has been flawed with a Eurocentric bias. For example, Eugen Strouhal's article on the Badarian morphology question is entitled "Evidence of the Early Penetration of Negroes into Predynastic Egypt."[5] Such a title assumes that "negroes" is a scientific term and that the indigenous people of Kemet were not Africans (blacks). The so-called "negroes" did not have to penetrate Egypt because the people of Kemet had "black skin and wooly hair."[6] Thus, even the Europeans who attempted to demonstrate a black presence in Egypt did so from the unscientific and racist premise that it was somehow exceptional that Africans occupied Africa. Strouhal's work, although published in the 1970s, is a direct theoretical descendant of what Bernal has called the Aryan model even though it is not Strouhal's intention to support that model. In effect, the negation of the model takes the model as reference point and is thereby as Eurocentric as the model itself.

My own analysis of Strouhal's work suggests an over-eager attempt to support an unsubstantiated thesis regarding ancient Egypt when most reputable scholars had abandoned the thesis as unsupported by the evidence. Strouhal's work is flawed in respect to the racial question. If one looks at the Badarians from the standpoint of German race theory where races were to constitute certain uniform characteristics rather than as gene pools that perhaps yield similar characteristics, it is possible to see how Strouhal could classify the 117 Badarian skulls he examined as being comprised of ninety-four mixed Negroid-Europoid, eight purely Negroid, and fifteen Europoid samples. Strouhal, however, is immediately in a quandary with the thesis he seeks to uphold. One could just as easily say that the 117 Badarian skulls he examined showed 102 were clearly Africoid while only fifteen showed any possibility of being related in morphology to Europoids. Furthermore, he admits that his examination included only the available Badarian skulls located in the Duckworth Laboratory at Cambridge (fifty-three skulls) and the Institute of Anatomy at Kasr El-Aini University of Cairo (sixty-four skulls).[7] Of course, this means that it is very difficult to draw any other conclusion about the morphology of the Badarians other than that in the limited sample they were overwhelmingly Africoid.

Strouhal's opening sentence contains all of the explosives which have surrounded classical African civilizations since the French invasions of the Nile Valley. Strouhal writes, "Theories about the Negro origin of the Ancient Egyptians have been with Egyptology ever since its beginnings."[8] Basing most of their early work on cranial theories, these Aryan modelers undertook to determine if Africans could truly have built the ancient civilizations of the Nile. Both Nubia and Kemet (Egypt) became the object of these craniometrists as they studied nasal and alveolar profile angles, nasal indices, indices of the ramus mandibulae, indices of the prominence of the nasal root (the height of the nasal root above the level of the anterior interorbital breadth), shape of the foreheads, nasal spines, and prominence of cheekbones. Such was the mad search to demonstrate that although Africans were prominent in the Nile Valley civilizations, they must have migrated there from some other place! In the face of Stouhal's questions about origin, Cheikh Anta Diop showed that the naturalistic statue of a woman made of ivory and discovered during the first excavation period (tomb 5107) was clearly African with her relatively broad nose.[9]

Neither Strouhal nor the more strident anti-African origin of civilization scholars can make any sense out of their positions. They want to say that the classical civilizations of the Nile Valley were not possible without European input. In the end, however, the argument loses ground on several counts. In the first place, when the Badarians settled in Kemet there was neither a Europe nor any knowledge of what a European was or was to become. There were, on the other hand, people of the continent of Africa. The Badarians, living on the continent, were clearly Africans.

The people are called Badarians after the village of Badari in southern Egypt where flint instruments, pottery, and other material evidences of one of the earliest African civilizations were found.

In the second place, Cheikh Anta Diop has proven conclusively that foreign elements in the Nile Valley were intruders, mainly from Asia. These people were often absorbed into the indigenous African population. Europeans are not present in any significant numbers prior to the 4th century B.C. Thus, the Badarians, who first appeared in the 4th millennia were indigenous Africans.

G. Brunton and G. Caton-Thompson reconstructed many details of Badarian life.[10] They contend that belief in the after-life first appears in Badarian ideology. Strouhal says that nose-rings and earrings appear to be of African origin because of the presence of such decorative jewelry pieces in the grave sites.[11] Other ideas attributed to the Badarians include astral and celestial worship, and ritual killing of the king in times of his decreased strength. Unquestionably, the basis of the religious, social, and decorative beliefs and practices of ancient Kemet are found in the early practices of the Badarians, who incidentally are everywhere acknowledged as an African, black civilization.

Albert Churchward and others have argued that the peopling of Europe and Asia was the direct result of African migration to those continents, a migration that occurred long before the development of Badarian civilization.[12] Indeed, it has been demonstrated that Sumerian civilization finds its origins in the African civilizations that preceded it.[13]

The Kemetic Legacy

The foundation of all African speculation in religion, art, ethics, moral customs, and aesthetics are derived from systems of knowledge found in ancient Egypt. To some extent it is this foundation, rather than the Greeks, that has made a lasting impact on the western world.

Egyptian Concepts in Other African Societies

We readily understand how Greek, for instance, has informed English with words like: meteorology, biography, biology, geology, aeronautics, astronomy, tragedy, comedy, elegiac, didactic, gramophone, drama, idea, theory, practice, philosophy, and ethical. Indeed, it would be difficult to discuss anything of significance in English without some deference to Greek.

The debt owed to classical Mdu Neter, pharaonic language, in other African societies is as extensive as the debt owed to Greek in some Western societies. Since the work in this area is only now beginning to be done linguistically we will rely almost entirely on the understanding of deeper and subtler meanings of ritual concept. Where it may not now be possible to establish a one-to-one correlation in a particular language with Mdu Neter, we are able to show concept similarity. Behind such similarity, of course, is the term or word that often remains undiscovered.

There are cases, however, where an African word from the Mdu Neter, e.g., "hbny," ebony, occurs in other African languages as well as European languages. Such was the significance of the classical African language that certain expressions leaped from the continent to Europe. The Kemetic heritage penetrates the literature, the orature, the pottery, the burial rituals, the procreative myths, and the modes of thought of Africa. It is the classical African civilizations themselves that have given us so much organic contact with the history of ideas. The vivid example of the massive memorials to African genius, Karnak, the temples of the Valley of the Kings, the Pyramids, the major shrines. When we feel, even now, the rhythms of creation in dance, art, literature, music, and talk the African intimacy with nature and fullness with life, we are experiencing our own standards, values, and codes exhibited in our approach to life thousands of years later. The festivals, the color, the vibrancy, the appeal to the deities, the incessant discussion, the dance, movement, show us ourselves dancing with the gods along the banks of the Nile.

During thousands of years of history prior to its struggle with outside influences, Kemet shaped and molded its distinctive mode of African civilization. It contrasted sharply with the crude customs of northern barbarians and the incipient cultures of the East. Kemet was pre-eminent in art, literature, astronomy, geometry, and ethics—all roads actually led to Kemet. The achievements of Kemetic genius are found in the civilizing role it played in Africa and the world. The Kemetic people seemed to reason about every aspect of human activity. They did not lose themselves in wonderment nor in idle self-congratulation but in intellectual and artistic pursuits that would govern human ideas for many centuries. If we were to state explicitly our debt to Kemet, we would have to say they gave us a sense of the possible. We owe to them the basis of science, art, ethical teachings, religion, dance, monarchy, and ritual drama.

I do not contend that Kemet was perfect, as some have claimed of ancient Greece, but that it was anterior in the design of the just and beautiful. There is no "mysterious perfection" in Kemetic architecture and art but rather the majestic combination of soul and beauty that produced the standards by which the world would follow. In ethical teachings as in art and science, we find that the works of the ancient Kemetic people are foundational for other cultures. In Arabic, for example, we find derivations from the ancient Kemetic language:

Kemetic	Arabic
Atum	Adam
Set	Satan
Hathor	Hajar
Ma'at	Ma'ad
Amun	Amen
Osiris	Asar

One might contrast the younger Greek art with Kemet by saying that whereas balance and symmetry became the central principles of Greek art, Kemetic art introduced measure, color, and right ordering of symbols as the premises for perfection. One sees this explicitly in the hieroglyphs, the elemental level of the Kemetic mind's rendering of the beautiful. No society had ever paid more attention to the placing of symbols and icons for aesthetic effect. What Kemet established remains the standard by which the African world and numerous other societies evaluate their artistic productions. Balance, timing, rhythm (right ordering), and color contrast are significant criteria for evaluation. Compared to Kemetic art and architecture, Greek expressions are simpler, less majestic, more austere.

It is no accident that with the conquest of Kemet by Alexander that the methods of Kemet passed to the Greeks. Consequently, the names of the sciences in most Western languages are now Greek names: mathematics, psychology, philosophy, biology, sociology, theology, meteorology, zoology, physics, physiology. This is the case although the first advances in the older sciences were made by Africans. Clearly philosophy was the most African of all of the early sciences. With Greek conquest came not only the subjugation of territory and people but the expropriation of ideas, concepts, and sciences. Herodotus says clearly that: "The names of nearly all of the gods came from Egypt to Greece."[14] But not only were the names of the gods taken by the Greeks but the complex of ideas, concepts, and temperaments that went with the deities. Thus, even where the name of the god may have become Greek over time, e.g., Thoth becoming Hermes, the ethical and moral qualities of the deities became the foundation for Greek mythology. Despite the difficulty in finding lasting political union or *pax Graeco* because they fought violently among themselves, the ancient Greeks, with the guidance of the relocated African deities, gave to the West a developing sense of human fellowship and a respect for the intangible qualities of artistic life.

Two natural phenomena have dominated African civilizations from the beginning: water and the sun. Ancient Kemet was the principal example of the roles played by these two natural phenomena. In every compartment of its cosmology, medicine, religion, agriculture and society these two decisive factors straddled the civilization like giant crocodiles.

The first was the Nile itself. A thread that kept pieces of the various kingdoms finely knitted, it generated monumental responses to the environment. The annual flooding made possible, as nowhere else, the necessity of calculations and predictions. In its powerful role as life giver the sun, like the river, came to represent well-being for the ancient Africans. I shall turn now to a more extensive discussion of each of the natural factors in their relationship to the society.

The River Nile

The central physical phenomenon of Egypt was the great river, the Nile. It played a vital role in the creation of Kemetic philosophy, agriculture, technology, and religion. The Africans called their land Kemet and it was designated "the land of the Blacks." This was quite appropriate inasmuch as the country had found its life from the emergence of civilization in Upper, that is, southern Egypt, where the people were often as black as the fertile soil that extended, on either side, the length of the Nile.

Without the mighty river, Egypt in ancient time would have been nothing but desert, an extension of the Great Sahara, barren and relatively lifeless. With the Nile, 4,000 miles long over its entire course, Egypt became a remarkable civilization. The river rises at the equator among the great lake and river system close to the majestic Zaire River. The Uganda Nile, as it can be called since it rises in Uganda, meets the Ethiopian Nile, or Abay River, near Khartoum. At this point the river is nearly 1,300 miles from the Mediterranean Sea.

Ancient Nubia, Ta-Seti, which covers portions of present-day Sudan and southern Egypt, shepherds the Nile through tortuous topography. In fact, there are six areas where the river passes through rough sandstone and limestone formations called cataracts. The valley of the Nile is gradually extended from ten to thirty miles in width as it passes through southern Egypt. A hundred miles from the Mediterranean Sea the Nile forms the Delta area which constitutes lower or northern Egypt proper. The Nile divides into two main branches. The western mouth is called Rosetta; the eastern mouth where the river empties into the sea is called the Damietta.

The Nile overflows each year, beginning around June. The Ethiopian Nile, Abay,is the source of the overflow because it carries the increased volume of water caused by melted snow into the Nile. By September or October the Nile reaches its peak. The regularity of this inundation aided the development of precision and gave the priests enormous responsibility and power because they could predict when the river would overflow. Hapi, the generous god of the annual flood, was honored for bringing joy to all human beings.

Much like other Africans in riverine areas of the continent the Egyptians viewed the world with security, stability and optimism. The world did not seem harsh and ferocious, cruel and menacing, to the Egyptian. To a large extent the geography of Egypt provided the people with a pleasant isolation except to the south. There were no harbors in the Delta, deserts east and west, and so openness to the south through the cataracts allowed Ethiopians and Nubians to interact with the Egyptians.

Irrigation, that is, the management of the water, provides a clue to the first grand project of a national or central character. Prior to and contemporaneous with the building of the pyramids was the emphasis on irrigation. The Egyptians built large rectangular basins to capture the overflowing waters. Silt was deposited in the basins and the Egyptians were able to use them for agricultural purposes.

Egypt represents the longest continuous African civilization in the ancient period. It lasted nearly four thousand years from about 4,000 B.C. to 332 B.C. Manetho, the Egyptian historian, wrote a book, *The History of Egypt*, under the Commission of one of the Greek kings, Ptolemy Philadelphus. This book is lost. Manetho's list of the thirty dynasties of ancient Egypt do exist, however. We are able to estimate the date of Menes' unification of the Lower and Upper kingdoms constituting the first dynasty of Egyptian history from Manetho's list. Some estimates are as late as 3,200 B.C. for Menes' conquest of Lower Egypt to unite the country. Regardless to the disagreement over the origin of the dynasties most experts admit that civilization existed in Egypt long before Menes combined the two regions and wore the United Crown. Dynastic Egypt introduced a powerful monarchy which lasted for thousands of years until it disintegrated with Alexander the Great's invasion of Africa.

The antiquity of Egypt creates problems of understanding because of the numerous breaks in the chain of dynasties, coups, foreign invasions and regional intrigues. Changes in religion, politics and art happened frequently enough to force Africanists and Africalogists to create their own periodizations. Large blocks of Egyptian history have been designated the Old Kingdom, Middle Kingdom, Empire, Ethiopian Period, Persian Period, and the Saitic Revival. I have renamed these periods: United Kingdom, Middle Kingdom, Majestic Period, Grand Empire, Persian Period, Saitic Revival, and Ptolemaic Rule.[15] Despite the modifications suggested by these periods the constancy and continuity of Egypt are remarkable for a country. The Egyptians retained their essential African outlook in terms of myths, symbolisms, and ethos throughout the history of the country. Only with the arrival of the Greeks and later in the seventh century A.D., the arrival of the Arabs in force did the mythopoeic pattern of Egypt undergo changes.

The pharaoh as deity always played a central role in Egypt's social and political life. Like the fixed role of the pharaoh was the major concepts of Egyptian life. Things did not change that much. The River Nile was predictable; the seasons came and went as they had been ordered by the gods, and life was stable, static; the only dynamic being the individual's quest to follow the priest's instructions for preparation for the afterward. Any dramatic change was certain to cause consternation. For example, if the Nile failed to overflow on time this would be an occasion of great discussion and contemplation leading to sacrifices to the riverine deities. Ancient Egyptians were convinced that the single most important fact was the changelessness of the cosmos. Thus, they believed in and relied upon the fixed nature of all human society.

A student of this classical African civilization must always note the struggle between the traditional and the innovative and see how tradition, whether in dance, agriculture, knowledge, or politics, gives little place to innovation. Ancient Egypt, like other classical African civilizations, placed a premium on the laws of the ancestors. Yet in its emphasis on tradition, Egypt perfected its pattern of governance and its reliance on static symbolisms.

This and the Thinite Era

Centered at This or Thinis in southern Egypt, near the city of Abydos, were temples and priests who directed the formative phase of early dynastic Egypt. This was the Timbuctoo of early dynastic Egypt. It attracted the leading scholars, warriors, and builders in the first two dynasties. At This it is now believed that hieroglyphic was developed as a sacred writing form. The first significant event the Africans recorded was the unification of Egypt by the mighty warrior-king, Menes, who is also called Narmer. Menes, a king of the south, subdued the kingdom of the north, as he had done with several smaller kingdoms in the south, and unified the country.

The "two lands" appears in Egyptian records to designate the historical, geographical, and cosmological significance of the act of uniting them. Egypt had been, prior to Menes, a double kingdom, and before that, a land of numerous independent clans. Some Egyptians even referred to Egypt after Menes as a double monarchy with a single king.

The crown of southern Egypt was a white crown. The crown of northern Egypt was a red crown. The white crown was called Hedjet; the red crown was called Deshert. At this, the new double crown was introduced and named Sekhemti. It united the two crowns and persisted throughout Egyptian history as the official royal crown.

The double crown, Sekhemti, represented a humanistic conquest where the conquering southerners allowed the crown of the northerners to flourish alongside theirs. Double offices were often maintained by the pharaoh; two actual set of palaces; two celebrations of the Sed festival for the coronation of the king, with distinctive insignia and ritual in each area; and two ceremonies for the king's burial in southern and northern Egypt.

Egyptian dualism was not based on history alone but cosmology. The Egyptians believed that an equilibrium of opposites was fundamental to everything. While it is true that nature, particularly in terms of the Nile and the climate, showed itself as the principle of harmony, in a ma'atic sense, the idea of appositional dualities found expression first in the universe itself; thus it was more celestial than fenestral. Some writers believe that the north-south, that is, lower-upper division of ancient Egypt was really seen in the light of a struggle between two gods, Seth of the north and Horus of the south. They place the history of the two lands in the context of strife. While strife often existed and frequently came out in the struggle for the Sekhemti, it is incorrect to interpret any Kemetic text in the light of regional antagonism, especially in relation to the gods Horus and Seth. Such interpretation owes more to contemporary realities than to ancient ones.

The Mighty Sun

The sun like the Nile was a dominant part of Kemetic life and thought. Its abundant heat and light produced in the people respect, awe, and inspiration. It influenced every aspect of Kemetic society. The fields did not give good crops without the sun, the well-being of the land was directly related to the sun, and so, the sun was also seen as a deity. It was at Heliopolis that the sun cult had its central influence although throughout Kemet there was a major association with the sun god.

Three forms of the sun god appeared in the two lands. At Atum the god was represented in human form wearing the red and white crowns of the two lands. At Heliopolis itself the sun god was often represented by a scarab beetle. The priests believed that the rising sun came forth like the scarab from its own substance and was reborn of itself. Thus, Khepra, the sacred scarab beetle, deposited its seed in tiny round pellets which were rolled with their back legs. To the Africans this was a perfect analogy to the movement of the sun across the sky. A third form of the sun god was as Ra with a human body and a falcon head. Crowned with a solar disc and a cobra, Ra gained preeminence by the Fifth Dynasty and was considered the head of the pantheon. Each morning, the Africans watched Ra slip from behind Manu, the Mountain of Sunrise, and sail across the sky, as it were, in his solar boat, accompanied by a divine retinue. As it true in other African societies such a powerful event had to be recorded as ritual drama. Dona Richards has claimed that ritual drama is at the heart of our spirituality.

In a mythopoeical manner at dawn the sun was a child represented by the scarab beetle Khepra; at midday he was an adult male represented by Ra; and at sunset he was Atum, an old man who disappeared into the horizon. The most mysterious part of all was the night voyage. By night he sailed through the underworld and made it just in time for the dawn trip across the sky. Nothing could be so certain. so consistent to the African as the journey of the sun.

Creation itself was believed to be the work of the sun god. When Atum was present alone in the watery mass of Nun which filled the universe, he generated two other gods by spitting them out. Thus, Shu and Tefnut, representing air and moisture, respectively, came forth. By their union Shu and Tefnut produced two children, Geb, the earth god and Nut, the sky goddess. Geb and Nut had four children, Osiris and Isis and Seth and Nephthys.

These nine deities constitute the Supreme Ennead who exercised control over the entire pantheon. Five of these deities are cosmological: Atum, Shu, Tefnut, Geb, and Nut. As the priests of ancient Kemet explained it, Geb (earth) and Nut (sky) were locked in a tight procreative embrace and Shu (air) came between them and pushed Nut skyward while Geb remained earthbound.

The other four deities were essentially involved in the relationship of the gods to human beings, especially through the office of the divine kingship. They were the major forces in society. Osiris represented the dead king and was always eternally resurrected in Horus, the living son. Seth, the implacable foe of Osiris, was the god of the deserts rather than the fertile lands. He was the Great Opponent who was abandoned by Nephthys, though his wife was able to assist Isis in sustaining Osiris. Atum does not figure as a major influence in this part of the order. His work is creation, not the maintenance, of society. Although it is true that the king, after

Chephren (ca. 2,900 B.C.E.), was considered a "son of Ra" the uraeus of the cobra goddess, Wadjyt, that appears on the king's forehead represents one symbol of Ra and shows the sun god's significance in the kingship though this is not a direct responsibility. The Supreme Ennead is in fact a corporate entity with two distinct functions although Atum sets them both in motion.

Interpreting the Kemetic Record

Africalogists can no longer study African societies as the carriers of detached, isolated, and quixotic culture separate from traditions. To do so is to commit a major intellectual crime inasmuch as the prototypes of the social/behavioral and cultural/aesthetic ideas and ideals found in discrete African societies and communities are connected to classical Africa. The scholar must at least explore the possibility that her or his research pursuit finds its source in a classical tradition. There are two reasons for this procedure: (1) re-confirmation and (2) delinking. Reconfirmation means that the scholar pursues the organic, Diopian unity of African thought, symbols, and ritual concepts to their classical origins. Delinking implies that the study of African phenomena ceases being a subset of the European intellectual project which maintains the study of African people, continental or diasporan, as marginal and peripheral.

An exploration, to be Africalogical, must be based on sound intellectual and philosophical foundations which maintain the centrality of the African experience and the primacy of the classical traditions. Whether the researcher is exploring African American child-rearing practices in North Philadelphia or African kinship patterns among the Galla in Ethiopia, reconfirmation and delinking are necessary steps in establishing the Afrocentric focus of the work. A researcher will find greater opportunity for reconfirmation or delinking in a given project but the process itself asserts the discipline in the research project.

A study of language in Africa, for example, must begin with the possibility of Diopian unity, interconnected graphic designs and philosophical continuity. Such has been the work of Theophile Obenga, Diop, Kagame, Carruthers and Karenga. Although these scholars have different emphases in their researches they all have utilized Afrocentric concepts.

Diop, Carruthers, and Karenga have claimed the primacy of the ancient Egyptian language as the beginning point for any real discussion about African studies.[16] In the wake of their proposals a whole new line of thinking has developed in the Afrocentric School of Thought; a line of thinking that was inherent, though not fully realized until now, in any fundamental examination of the nature of scholarship about African people. Egypt was indeed the light of Africa and Africa the light of Egypt, as Diop had maintained.

These scholars have maintained that without connecting all African studies to classical African civilizations and cultures our research remains essentially tangential and peripheral. As a Diopian Afrocentricist I have found the arguments of these writers convincing and compelling. Therefore, I have attempted to advance the line of thinking, based upon my own studies of the ancient language of Egypt, Mdu Neter, by examining the various transformations of the classical language in other African languages and indeed in the languages of Europe as well. This becomes necessary in light of the many distortions of African culture and history that appear in the writings of European scholars who began their work in the womb of a racist ideology. Their entire point of view toward Africa was negative and few of the early Egyptologists could divorce their hegemonic attitudes towards knowledge about other people from their political position in the world.

It is their political positions that have created the tremendous misunderstanding regarding the African presence in world history. Almost all of the Eurocentric writers, e.g., Breasted, Lichtheim, Budge, Piankoff, and DeBuck, among others, saw Egypt as a part of some mysterious "oriental" culture entirely unrelated to the continent where it was situated. They went so far as to devise complex explanations for the separation of Egypt from the rest of Africa. The Nile River was seen as a barrier because of the cataracts; the desert was called a natural barrier to Egypt's contact with its neighbors to the South and West; and the relationship of Egypt to Syria looms larger than its relationship to Ethiopia in the minds of these Eurocentric writers.

Carruthers identifies three fundamental faults in the thinking of the Eurocentric Egyptologists: (1) they confused "Nhsi" and "ha," (2) they failed to understand the subtleties of the ancient language and employed European concepts to African behaviors, and (3) they failed to understand the "dramatic meanings beneath the formal and obvious meanings" in the ancient texts.[17] In any interpretation of the connection between African social and cultural systems the lack of a basic perspective centered on Africa itself is problematic. For example, as Carruthers points out, the eminent African thinkers Chancellor Williams and DeGraft-Johnson made incorrect analyses based upon their reliance of the mistranslations of the Mdu Neter texts by white Egyptologists.[18] These scholars accepted the translation of "nhsi" as "Negro" a racial distinction, rather than see that the ancient Africans of Egypt would never make such a distinction between themselves and the Africans who lived to the South and West of them. The Eurocentric Egyptologists only interpreted "nhsi" as "Negro" out of their own perspective toward reality. They lived and wrote during a time when racial distinctions were very much a part of the social landscape. Even today some white Egyptologists try to distinguish between Egyptian and other Africans as if to say Egypt is not in Africa. But "nhsi" represents the varied features of the Egyptians as well as other Africans. All one has to do is to look at the murals, the engravings, and statuettes which provide abundant physical evidence of the antiquity of Egypt's Africanity. The people of ancient Egypt were no different than the African people of the United States, Brazil, Mali, Nigeria, Ethiopia, Sudan, or Zimbabwe. Carruthers contends emphatically that "the linguistic data settle the argument, Nhsi is not a race or color distinction but a national distinction since the word for Black in the context of color is 'Km' which is the root of the word which the Egyptians called themselves."

The problem of the subtleties of the language has been adequately dealt with by Karenga in his retranslation *The Husia* which represents the best example to date of a systematic attempt to infuse the translations of the ancient texts with African as opposed to European concepts.[20] Karenga is profoundly historical in his approach to the texts and although this has engendered a certain amount of criticism, he is correct to assume, as he does, that any antihistorical hostility is due to an incomplete understanding of the process of Afrocentric reconstruction. Our analysis, therefore, of the connections between the ancient Egyptian language and other African languages must be organic and historical. This brings us to the problem of the Rosetta Stone mythology itself. Given to the world as the key to ancient Egypt, the Rosetta Stone myth starts with Napoleon's Army in 1799. Actually, the build up for the Rosetta Stone myth starts with 1638 when John Greaves drew up the measurements of the Great Giza Pyramid. In the eighteenth century Richard Pococke studied the Dahshur and Sakkara sites, attempting to make scientific measurements of the various groups of monumental works. But it was Napoleon's Army, like the army of Alexander of Macedonia nearly 2,000 years earlier, that shocked the world of ancient Egyptian studies. While Alexander's army had raided the libraries and museum and taken the books to Athens, Napoleon's army, probably remembering the great bounty taken by armies before, had several authors and would-be-scholars among the soldiers.

Dominique-Vivant Denon accompanied Napoleon's General Desaix on his campaign into Upper Egypt and was totally over-whelmed by the monuments of this classic African civilization. Dominique-Vivant Denon saw it as the most fabulous sight human eyes had even seen. Nothing in Greece or Italy compared to what the savant saw in Upper Egypt. In 1803 he published his book *Description de l'Egypt*. The Jomard group of publishers immediate-ly found it successful and the work became a standard as it opened up a new field of study. Dominique-Vivant Denon illustrated his work with meticulous drawings and the European world that had basked in the glories of Greece and Rome realized that there was a far older and grander civilization of which they knew little. Since the script and the language of Egypt was African, and "exotic," Europeans felt intense competition to decipher the script. It was like an enormous criminal case in which the police detectives had to deliver a suspect, had to break open the case, had to show that the case was not beyond their powers of deciphering. It is easy to understand this social and racial pressure on the scholars and writers of Europe.

Thus, during the same campaign in which Dominique-Vivant Denon had found his inspiration, one of the engineers of Napoleon's army is said to have found the Rosetta Stone. This stone became the possession of the British Museum after France's withdrawal from Egypt. But the British did not move it to London before casts had been made and Champollion was able to decipher the script. Upon Champollion's "break-through" in 1822 the European world went wild with excitement. Then in 1828-29 Champollion led an expedition to Egypt for eighteen months in order to copy inscriptions. The Germans soon followed the British and French with scholars and plunderers. In fact, the twelve-volume work on Egyptian monuments that was the basis of the great Berlin collection was paid for by the Prussian government. Auguste Mariette was sent by the Louvre to collect Egyptian antiquities and soon received authority to establish the Egyptian Museum and Antiquities Service, becoming its first director. This gave the Europeans direct access to the entire field of African classical arti-facts and would make the task of overturning erroneous interpreta-tions, based on ethnocentric interests, doubly difficult. William Matthew Flinders Petrie was the first person to hold a chair of Egyptology in England at the University College, London. This chair had been founded by the wealthy Amelia Edwards, who wanted very much to be the major player in this part of African research. She set up the Egypt Exploration Fund and this was later followed by the Deutsche Orient Gesellschaft and the Mission Archeologique Française which became the Institut Français d'Archeologie Orientale.

Already in the late 1880s the European scholars had decided to place Egypt in the Orient, that is, Egyptian Studies was to become a branch of Oriental Studies, not African Studies. The European creation of Oriental Studies and the inability to see Africa in the light of its ancient past meant that the degradation of the African was nearly complete. Few European scholars could see Kemetic civilization as African in the nineteenth century. Although "oriental" has come to mean to the Europeans "Islamic" as well as Japan, India, and China, there was no such confusion in African antiquity. The Nile Valley civilizations predate Arab conquest and represent the indigenous developments of the Africans. The Berlin

Conference of 1884-85 underscored the condition of all of Africa as the European powers divided up the continent among themselves without a thought to the democratic rights of the peoples in the various territories. All of the plundering and raiding of ancient monuments and sites in Africa could happen because of two important facts.

The first is the complete abandonment of the classical African civilizations by the conquering Arabs from the seventh century to the eighteenth century. With limited exceptions the Arabs controlled the whole of North Africa from the first jihads out of Arabia in 641. They appeared to have little respect or appreciation for the classical civilization they found in the Nile Valley. Having destroyed the organic structure of the African society they found in Egypt, reinstituted the ban on the Egyptian language, and allowed the great ancestral holy places to lie in ruin, the Arabs created the perfect opportunity for the distortion of the African heritage of Egypt. As the second reason for this state of affairs in Egyptian studies, the subsequent suppression of the Arabs by the Ottoman Turks and Europeans made it possible for the colonizers to dictate the terms of the study of ancient Egypt, even to assume the leadership of the antiquities services.

As African people were colonized and enslaved both on the continent and in the Americas, there were few voices raised against the appropriation of African history as there were few voices raised against the appropriation of our land and labor. Just as we had to throw off the yoke of oppression from our bodies and our lands we will have to liberate the study of the classical civilizations because the European colonization of geography, that is, land, went hand-in-hand with the colonization of information and knowledge. Visit any museum in any major European city and there you will see the great treasures of Africa, taken over a five-hundred-year period. Read any book on African people and you will see the robbing of African civilization, history, and culture. This is why it seems in most European works that African peoples had no culture, no history, no dynamism prior to European domination and exploitation. A people's classical history is important for the reason that it forms a part of the grand continuity of concepts, values, experiences, visions, and possibilities. Having separated Egypt from Africa in their minds, the Eurocentric Egyptologists began the process of making African societies, other than Egypt, static entities that never changed over time. This was in some ways an intellectually criminal act because it violated the best traditions of evidence and beyond that it violently detached a part of the continent from the rest of the continent.

The Europeans were certainly not alone in this process. The history of Ibn Khaldun is a significant example of the historiography of the conqueror.[21] Although the Khaldunic history provides some interesting viewpoints from the fourteenth century about Africa it is nonetheless a historiography of conquest of the African peoples. The Berbers, Tuaregs, Shilluks, and Nuer who fought to keep their territories in the face of the onslaught of Islamic armies do not even receive footnotes in the Khaldunic version of history.[22] In fact, it is these people "without history" who have played major roles in the transforming phenomena of the African continent. Their histories, once told, will fill in the cultural and linguistic gaps as well as the linkages between the various African nations and kingdoms. As late as the 1890s Azande kings were refusing to wear Arab clothes, preferring to wear the leopard-skin as an insignium of royalty.[23] An important Azande king like Mdarama found the Arab clothing imposed upon his culture to be a violation of his traditions well into the 1890s. Of course, as in other matters, the conquerors soon had their way and the Azande adopted both Arab and European styles before the twentieth century was in full swing. Even so, it is the history of people like the Azande, the Nubians, the Dinka, the Shilluk, and the Sara who will provide us the linguistic keys to the ancient Nile Valley's connection to the rest of Africa.

In such an exploration of cultural factors it is necessary to make some primary interpretations. Because of our Diopian orientation we are certain to make different interpretations from those imposed by European tradition. For example, the Nuer refer to Kwoth as the principal deity in their culture. Kwoth is the guide of the human race; Kwoth manages the affairs of the Nuer through attention to the rules of nature; and Kwoth is the measurer of a person's life. In every respect Kwoth is like Thoth, Tehuti, the Kemetic deity who became known as the father of writing and as the deity who taught the world to keep records. Kwoth, to the Nuer, a people close enough to the ancient cradle of the religion of Kemet in Nubia to have connections, linguistically and culturally, to the ancient people, is clearly related in linguistic structure to Thoth. Since few Europeans knew anything about African societies prior to the fifteenth century they could not see any connections between people they came to enslave and the classical societies of the African continent. Thus, almost every study of an African society begins in the nineteenth century, whether it is Kuper studying the Swazi, Evans-Pritchard studying the Azande, or Rene LeMarchand studying the Batutsi or Bahutu.

The fact that they do not go back farther than they do means two things: (1) they have no interest in attaching the rest of Africa to Egypt, and (2) they see African societies as detached, static, and isolated from intracontinental interaction. Such a construction has disconnected Africa from its classical civilizations. Almost nowhere in Europe's intellectual conceptualization or in its "approach" to Africa has the continent been conceived of holistically. In fact, all European training in research methodology has left scholars devoid of an Afrocentric perspective. African Studies in the West is, too often, a Eurocentric enterprise still pursued according to the dictates of sixteenth-century hegemonic thinking.

Thus, one finds a writer like Albert Hyma who was knighted by the Dutch Queen Wilhelmina for his work in Dutch history, making the following statement in his *Ancient History*:

> It is clear to all historians that Europe was originally barbarous, and when it finally emerged out of barbarism to receive the first gifts of civilized life, they were transmitted to the Europeans by the inhabitants of the ancient Near East [*sic*]. We know now that the first homes of civilized man were Mesopotamia [*sic*] and Egypt. Between 3500 and 2500 B.C. the extreme southeastern part of Europe was illuminated by the culture of ancient Egypt and Mesopotamia. After this region had basked for a time in the light of Oriental (sic, read African) civilization, barbarians swooped down from the north, destroyed part of the

highly civilized life they found there, and then became
civilized in turn.[24]

It is possible to forgive Hyma for some of his sins because much of
what we know about the ancient world now was not known when
he first began to write. We now know, for example, that the first
cities in history were not developed in Mesopotamia by the Sumerians around 4500 B.C. but rather in the region of the Nubian desert
in northern Sudan and Southeastern Egypt around 20,000 B.C. Data
first recorded by the United States Columbia shuttle in 1978 point
to buried cities under the desert. These settlements represent the
first known communities where human beings organized societies
according to skills and specialties. Scientists believe that these
settlements predate any that have been discovered so far. What is
unforgivable in Hyma's conceptualization of ancient history is the
idea that Egypt is in the Orient. Clearly this is the bias of categorization created initially in the nineteenth century and maintained in
the present century by institutions such as the School for Oriental
and African Studies in London and the various other "Oriental"
institutes set up in Europe and the United States. So while Hyma
could admit, as he did, that Europe received from Egypt "its
earliest knowledge of civilized life" he could not admit that Egypt
was African.[25] In fact, in a telling paragraph, Hyma concludes of
the paintings of Egyptians "Their skin had been white, but powerful rays of the sun quickly turned the color to tan."[26] Whatever is
meant by this statement, it seems clear that Hyma denies the blackness of the ancient Egyptians, a fact that has been established
scientifically by the leading Egyptologists of the contemporary era,
Theophile Obenga and the late Cheikh Anta Diop.[27]

The heresy of the eighteenth, nineteenth, and twentieth century
European writers in regards to the Egyptians was never in the mind
of the Greeks, the earliest classical writers of Europe. Indeed, the
Greeks saw Egypt, an African country, as the cradle of wisdom and
knowledge. The most famous of the Hellenes crossed the sea to be
initiated, if they could, at the temples of Egypt. Such was the
attraction of this center of information and culture for the Greeks,
Sicilians, and Persians. Even the most quintessential Greek figures,
such as Orpheus and Homer, are said to have travelled to Egypt.[28]

Both Solon and Plato crossed the Mediterranean to pay their homage to ancient Egypt.[29] Thales, Pythagoras, Oenopidus, and Eudoxus are only a few of the early Greek thinkers who found it necessary to study in Africa. Indeed, according to Diogenes Laerce in *Thales* we find that Thales learned his astronomy and geometry from the Egyptian priests.[30] We also know from the Greeks that Pythagoras spent twenty two years in the temples of Egypt.[31] Olympiodorus in his *Life of Plato* and Strabo in his description of Egypt say that Plato spent thirteen years in Egypt learning geometry and theology.[32] The celebrated writers of Greece became more popular if they could proclaim they had been educated by the priests in Africa.

There is no great emphasis in the period prior to the eighteenth century for taking Egypt and Nubia out of Africa and making those ancient civilizations "oriental" if they could not be European. Therefore, it is obvious that the predicament of Africa, the great European commerce in human slavery, and the need to minimize the contribution of Africans in order to justify the institution of slavery meant that the European writers would deliberately falsify historical records. In many ways they participated in a vulgar scholarship culminating in the works of the famous servant of Eurocentric scholarship on Africa, Sir E. A. Wallis Budge. Budge was the chief "Egyptologist" of the British Museum at a time when "orientalism" was at its highest level. Budge brought the work of Barthelemy to fruition in his many projects. As Keeper of the Egyptian and Syrian Antiquities in the museum Budge made his career on interpretations, translations, Karenga says "mistranslations," and reproduction of the Egyptian pieces.[33]

Many books on Egypt bear his name. Budge became famous for his work on *Dwellers on the Nile*, *Egyptian Magic*, *The Gods of the Egyptians*, *Osiris and the Egyptian Resurrection*, and *The Egyptian Book of the Dead*. Thus the scholar who wants to explore the possibilities of African connections, African philosophy, or African culture must first venture through the maze created by Budge and others such as James Breasted of the University of Chicago.[34]

Budge's assessment of the importance of the Rosetta Stone, once a source of mystery and intrigue among many Egyptian scholars, is an astounding exposure of the European attitude toward African language. The Rosetta Stone, now in the British Museum's Egyptian Gallery, was the source of enormous controversy when it was first brought to Europe. During the French campaign in Egypt, a French artillery officer found the Rosetta Stone in the ruins of Fort St. Julien, near the Rosetta mouth of the Nile. To understand the full significance of this rather ordinary-looking four-foot-long stone it is important to grasp the known facts of its generation. The stone was apparently made to record the activities of Ptolemy V. Epiphanes, a representative of the Greek, Alexander of Macedonia. Ptolemy ruled the land from 205 to 182 B.C.E.

The stone contains information on the many projects carried out by Ptolemy V. Epiphanes, the gratitude expressed to him by the priests who ordered that statues of the king be placed in the temples of Egypt, and that copies of the decree be made on basalt stelae and set up in temples near the king's statues. The Rosetta Stone is taken to be one of the stelae that was supposed to be made in honor of the decree. Questions could be raised regarding the historical veracity of this account which appears on the stone. So far only one of these several stones has been recovered despite the fact that they were to be set up in three temples.

Budge is quick to point out that the real value in the stone lies in its philological importance because it opens the door to understanding ancient Egyptian.[35] This was the key to deciphering the great body of African literature that had come down through the centuries. In fact, Budge says in his typically Eurocentric manner, "until the beginning of the last century there was neither an Oriental nor a European who could either read or understand a hieroglyphic inscription."[36] It is absolutely awesome to think that the Europeans never thought of examining African languages and graphics, since they were examining Egyptian, for connections to the ancient language. Mdu Neter is related to many other African languages both in its structure and in its ideographs. The only reason one can give for this blatant disregard for the languages of the people on the continent itself is the pervasive attitude that Africans did not create ancient Egypt. The Europeans of the Aryan school were willing to look to the Syrians, the Phoenicians, the

Indians, and the Arabs before they turned their eyes to the neighbors of Egypt in Africa for linguistic or cultural relatedness.

Meanwhile, white writers, prior to the European recovery of the Rosetta Stone, wrote preposterous interpretations of the ancient language. Some said that every word was a biblical expression, others claimed that Hebrew compositions were found on the temple walls, and still others said that the hieroglyphics were alphabetic characters but it is not until Champollion, a student of Coptic and an avid believer in the value of parallel linguistic, published a piece on the meaning of a red granite obelisk found by J. W. Bankes in 1815 and set up in Dorsetshire, England, that some real progress was made. This is not to say that others had not been on the road to deciphering the ancient language. Certainly the work of Akerblad, Zoega, and Young are names that must be mentioned in conjunction with the project. However, it is Champollion who saw that the obelisk had Greek and Egyptian inscriptions and that one of the names was Ptolemy. He was able to read Ptolemy in both Greek and hieroglyphics and this made him believe that he could interpret the Rosetta Stone if he could discover the exact meaning of the Greek. So when he had examined the obelisk and found one of the names on it that he had seen on the Rosetta Stone he was certain that he had the key. The fact that the first translations were done by non-Afrocentrists underscores why Africalogists should study the language.

Carruthers contends that the mastery of the ancient language is a major enterprise for African scholars.[37] He states that "we should use that language as our classical language just as the Europeans use Greek and Latin today."[38] Obenga has placed the issue of ancient Egyptian as the classical language of Africa at the front door of linguistic research in Africa: "*Cette question est la véritable question de la recherche linguistique aujourd'hui en Afrique.*"[39] It must also be placed on the front burner of our own work because it is impossible to reestablish historical and cultural linkages without first understanding the relationship of present behavior to the classical concepts. All language defines the users.

When the Europeans first entered the arena of modern Egyptian studies we were little equipped to make our own researches. Fortunately, the new impetus in Egyptian studies comes from

African scholars convinced that the secret to all African culture is through the door of Kemet. In fact, the Africalogist brings to such study the community or circle of memory, openness to a wide range of African scholarship, not centered on a small isolated village or group, but rather broad and multidisciplinary perspectives from an Afrocentric angle, and a commitment to excellence. Scholars of the Association for the Study of Classical African Civilizations are rich in linguistics, historical, anthropological, sociological, political theory and cultural analysis backgrounds; some of the writers have special capabilities in philosophy and ethics. This means that the advances to be made in classical civilizations will be made by many of these writers and scholars. Their work in Africa itself, their mastery of the languages of the continent, and their commitment to the African Cultural Project will ensure understanding the generative power of the Kemetic chronology.

KEMETIC CHRONOLOGICAL TABLE

Foundation of the Empire

(First Dynasty 3500-2890 B.C.)

Narmer (Menes)
Aha
Djer
Den
Semerkhet
Qaa

(Second Dynasty 2890-2686 B.C.)

Hotepsekhemwi
Nynetjer
Peribsen
Khasekhemwi

First Golden Age

(Third Dynasty 2686-2613 B.C.)

Sanakhte
Zoser
Sekhemkhet
Huni

(Fourth Dynasty 2613-2494 B.C.)

Sneferu
Cheops
Chephren
Micerinus

(Fifth Dynasty 2494-2345 B.C.)

Userkafi
Sahure
Nyuserre
Unas

(Sixth Dynasty 2345-2181 B.C.)

Teti
Pepi I
Merenre
Pepi II

First Period of Instability

This was the time of the first period of political instability which lasted from 2181 to about 2133 B.C. The
period included the 7th to 10th Dynasties.

Second Golden Period

(Eleventh Dynasty 2133-1991 B.C.)

Mentuhotep I

Inyotef I-III
Mentuhotep II-IV

(Twelfth Dynasty 1991-1786 B.C.)

Amenemet I
Sesostris I
Sesostris III
Amenemet III

(Thirteenth Dynasty 1786-1633 B.C.)

Sebekhotep III
Neferhotep

Second Period of Instability

A second period of political unrest in which Kemet
was governed in part by the Asiatic Hyksos. The
fourteenth, fifteenth, sixteenth and seventeenth dynasties consisted of intermittent rule by Hyksos and
indigenous rulers.

New Kingdom

(Eighteenth Dynasty 1567-1320 B.C.)

Amosis
Amenophis
Tuthmosis I
Tuthmosis II
Hatshepsut
Tuthmosis III
Amenophis II
Tuthmosis IV
Amenophis III
Akhenaton
Smenkhkare

Tutankhamen
Ay
Horemheb

(Nineteenth Dynasty 1320-1200 B.C.)

Rameses I
Seti I
Rameses II
Merneptah
Amen-meset
Seti II

(Twentieth Dynasty 1200-1085 B.C.)

Sethnakhte
Rameses III
Rameses IV-XI

Third Period of Instability

The third great period of political instability occurred between 1166 B.C. and 750 B.C. This was a time of family rivalries, jealousies, disorganization in foreign policy and lack of vision.

Third Golden Period

(Twenty-fifth Dynasty 750-656 B.C.)

Piankhi
Shabaka
Taharka
Shabataka

(Twenty-sixth Dynasty 664-525 B.C.)

Psammetichus I
Necho II
Apries
Amasis

The Decline of the Great Kingdom
(From 526 B.C. to 50 B.C.)

The Twenty-seventh Dynasty consisted of Assyrian conquering kings, and the Twenty-eighth-Thirtieth Dynasties of the last indigenous Kemetic rulers. After this period came the invasion of the Macedonians and the Ptolemaic Dynasty named after Alexander's general, Ptolemy. The Romans took Kemet from the Greeks and made it a part of the Roman Empire.

Kemet provides us with the richest sources of ancient African ideals and concepts, thereby giving the Africologist an entirely new bases for developing theory. However, the question of civilization is always raised in conjunction with the question of writing. While Kemet gives us the clear example of Mdu Neters as a language form, we are often confused as to the meaning of this for other parts of Africa.

The Writing Question

Two problems have existed in previous interpretations of African graphic systems: (1) The conscious attempt to isolate Egypt, Ethiopia and Meroe (Nubia) from the rest of Africa, and (2) the promulgation of the view that Africans never invented writing systems.[40] Both of these problems find their source in the condescending attitudes of Eurocentric authors whose purposes, economic or religious, found no place for a genuine analysis of the writing systems of Africa. Most of the early European authors were missionaries seeking to understand "primitive" languages in order to bring us into the more perfect light of European religion.

The rise of human civilization in the Nile Valley of northeast Africa is pretty much agreed upon by reputable scholars.[41] Today, no one questions the anteriority of the African civilization of that region. Since human civilization carries with it certain necessary relational skills and functions, it is reasonable to assume that these early Nile Valley civilizations possessed some form of writing, some method of transmitting ideas. It would be impossible to expand culture without some communication system. While the oral communication system predates the visual system, the impact of Egypt, Axum, and Nubia, as recipient cultures of the earlier visual forms, found expression on the walls and in the furniture and domestic artifacts of cultures in other parts of Africa.[43]

The word script refers to a system of visual symbols used to communicate, record, and entertain. A script conforms to an established convention if it is to be meaningful and functional and script is comprised of units called "mdus," that is, the smallest single units of the script system.[44] Other authors choose to use different labels for the smallest single unit of script. I have merely employed the logical system of using concepts from the most ancient classical African language available.

Three major distinguishable writing systems exist in Africa: (1) pictograms, (2) ideograms, and (3) syllabic scripts. The pictogram is written (drawn, painted, shaped) on human skin, walls, mud, sand, metal, bark or paper, in a manner representative of some object of the visual world. It is therefore not considered abstract. Throughout Africa one can find, as I have found, great variation in pictograms. These pictograms often form sequential stories, or warnings, or greetings. The area of central Africa, encompassing Zaire, Gabon, Cameroons, and the Central African Republic are particularly rich in pictogrammatic expressions. The *bwiti* religious symbolism in Gabon, the painted house walls of western Cameroons, or the specially carved naturalistic picture sequences often used in Malawi by the *sing'anga*, doctor, to greet his clients constitute narrative examples of the pictogram. Examples of this form can be found in almost all African societies.

The ideogram is written (drawn, shaped, painted, carved) on various materials and is used to state an idea. Thus, the perceptible word is represented in this manner. Among the Akan several ideograms are often used to state highly complex ideas.[45] This, of course, is an extensive graphic form in Africa. Some authors claim the difference between ideographs and pictograms reside in the fact that the pictogram is more literal, showing less abstraction. Therefore the pictographs relationship to an object is direct, easily transmitted by virtue of its literalness. On the other hand the ideogram, where it is related to a concrete object, is usually symbolic, that is, the object represents something other than itself. So culturally based are most ideograms that an individual would normally have to be instructed in the meaning of the ideograms in order to read. For example, the Chinese ideogram for "happy" combines elements which show a mother and son, since this is the happiest relationship in Chinese traditional culture.

In the ancient Egyptian language, ideograms came to represent profound philosophical concepts. Thus, Anubis was shown with the face of a dog and came to be known as the one who accompanies the dead to the next world. Horus, son of Isis and Osiris, was written as a falcon-headed god, while Thoth (Tehuti), the father of writing, appeared as an ibis with a writing palette in his hand. Without an appreciation for Mdu Neter, the ancient Egyptian language, it will be difficult to understand the ideograms.

Ideographs in Africa

Nsibidi is an ideographic script that has come under close scrutiny in recent years because of its wide provenance as a graphic system. It is a graphic system used by various philosophico-socio societies in east-central Nigeria to communicate philosophy.[46] But it is not as Kubik says "a secret graphic system."[47] At one time nsibidi flourished among the Ibo and Edo as well as the Efik people, who are now the keepers of the script. Its considerable antiquity, confirmed by several scholars, suggests that its philosophical content may have come from the convergence of several systems. In fact, the thesis, expounded by several scholars, that ancient Egyptian priests and their traditions returned to the central region of Africa with the coming of the Arab jihads is significant in this regard. It means that nsibidi is connected to the origin of the African philosophic system since similar writing appears throughout Africa. We know now that every region of the continent had some form of script long before the missionaries, slave traders and settlers came to pillage and distort. In Angola and Zambia, an ideographic system called sona is practiced by several ethnic groups, including the Cokwe, Lucazi, Mbwela, and Mbunda. In the Cokwe language the system is called sona; in the other languages it is tusona. Unlike nsibidi, a system for philosophical knowledge, sona also transmits empirical mathematics. The recent work of Kubik and Jaritz attest to the prominence of this system in south central Africa.[48] Numerous people use ideographic writing in the sand as means of warning, information, and leisure mathematic play. Hunters, returning to their village, often stop to make ideographic mathematic puzzles in the sand of a dry river bed.[49]

The Akan people of Ghana and the Ivory Coast have a tradition of djayobwe, bronze figures used for weighing gold, that are graphic, either in a pictograph or an ideograph form. The dja are indigenous to Ghana, Ivory Coast and Togo. Niangoran-Bouah says all the elements of the dja, both figurative and geometrical, are weights.[50] These forms, while local in their provenance, have philosophical connections and conceptual relationship to other symbolic forms in Africa. It is clear from historical records that the Akan came from the Sahara region.[51] Insofar as black autochthonous groups are found in Morocco, Libya, Algeria and Tunisia, we can speculate that the interlinking of conceptual ideas have existed for millennia throughout West Africa.[52] The masked figures in the cave paintings of the Sahara Desert show that the region belonged to black people in the Neolithic Period before it became desert and as Niangoran-Bouah says "The Sahara belongs to Black Africa."[53] So the value of the djayobwe in a discussion of the graphic systems of Africa is the linkage to the ancient classical civilization of Egypt.[54]

Phonological Scripts

The most prominent phonological scripts, those that represent the sounds of a language, are Vai, Toma, Mende and Bamun in Liberia, Guinea, Sierra Leone and Cameroons. When Europeans first examined African writing systems they looked for the phonological systems because these held greater similarity to their own systems. Phonological systems are either alphabetical like English or syllabic like Japanese. In any case the script corresponds to a certain sound. Examining Africa from a Eurocentric viewpoint they concluded that there were no written languages in Africa until the nineteenth century. All serious researchers have now abandoned that preposterous thesis. It was an extravagant thesis, at any rate, because the ancient Meroitic text, the Ge'ez of Ethiopia, and the ancient Egyptian systems of writing predated any European system.

There is a political dimension to script preference which resides in the nature of the script. Since phonological scripts are language dependent they tend to maximize standardization and expansion. On the other hand, pictographs and ideographs are language independent and although they may be understood, like Chinese, by many people, they are not necessarily efficient. The great number of characters means that any form of duplication becomes problematic whereas in English the idea is to eliminate smaller dialects and have a one-to-one correlation between a unit of script and pronunciation.

The question of which script is the most "civilized" has also occupied the European mind. Once those who subscribe to what Martin Bernal has labeled the Aryan School accepted that Africans have graphic writing, then the question becomes, is it the highest form? As Kubik maintains "The nature and character of a graphic system used in a specific culture depends so much on the needs of that particular culture at a certain time, that its existence may also be explained functionally."[55]

Example of Scripts

Written scripts, whether as pictograms, ideograms, or phonological scripts are not the only means of sending a message. The "object script" is also widely used in Africa, and has been, at least, since predynastic Egypt. The object script is when a communicator uses a certain object in a particular way to send messages. For example, the placing of stones in a special arrangement, the breaking of sticks, or the twisting of fabric can all be used to convey messages. This form of communication crossed the West African sea (the Atlantic Ocean) to find a home in the Americas. Enslaved Africans often found escape routes by "reading" the object scripts of twisted branches or pieces of cloth left by others. On the continent itself, especially in West Africa, object scripts have been used by young boys or girls to mark access to their secret places.

There are several African object scripts that serve as mnemonic systems. Among the Yoruba we find the arókò, a highly complex way of sending a message used by military leaders, kings, and princes. It is usually a string of cowrie shells twisted with feathers into various configurations. Theophile Obenga found that arókò could be a simple symbolic message or an elaborately structured system of cowrie shells.[56] He also found that each arrangement of cowries and feathers represented one word. Thus it was possible that in reading a message one had to articulate the number of cowries like syllables. Kubik says "Arókò is an ingenious system, mnemonic, but at the same time phonetic, a form of 'script without paper.'"[57] Arókò is not the only practical system of object scripts. Mekutu alélé of Cameroons, ngombo of Angola are two of the major object scripts using carved objects placed in some kind of divining bowl.

Kubik has raised an important issue regarding these object scripts. He is correct to see that the issue as to whether or not these object scripts can be called graphic or script resides in the nature of the European question.[58] In European languages script has a strong Latin background (escrito, Portuguese; ecriture, French; shrift, German) and particular referenta. Yet the concept in African languages has its own specific terminology and categories. Consequently a cultural analyst should not force African fields into European definitions. I do not accept a narrow definition for script. That imposes a European particularism on African language behavior.

Africans were the first human beings to "script" as a matter of communicative record. The ancient Egyptians left the most extensive and impressive records of antiquity. We know almost all that we know of dynastic Egypt because of the ideograms and pictograms which first appeared around 6,000 B.C. Almost as early as the Egyptians were the Sumerians whose cuneiform syllabic script system written in soft clay, gives us another ancient view.[59] The Egyptian hieroglyphic system, however, lasted much longer and can be traced in various scripts of Africa. The alphabetic script emerged around 2,000 B.C. in Asia and spread to Europe.

The Eurocentric evolutionist theories postulated High and Primitive cultures. In such a formulation all African civilizations, with the possible exceptions of Egypt and Axum, were considered "primitive" cultures. These designations were often made on the basis of either the lack of permanent architecture or the lack of a writing system. But since definitions tend to be based on the position and perspective of the person doing the defining, the European scholar often looked at Europe, what he knew, and tried to use it as a standard for evaluating other cultures. Thus, African societies, when they were no longer considered "primitive" were termed "simple" as opposed to "complex." Europeans societies were considered "advanced" and more "complex" than African societies, a sort of evolution in explanatory theories.

The implications of this view are numerous. In the first place it means that pictographs are considered the simplest forms of writing. Ideographs are more complex and finally the ultimate stage is the phonological script which lead directly to alphabetical scripts.

Although several writers have examined in some detail the emergence and development of writing in Africa, there remains, largely because of the surrogate racist categorization of Levy-Bruhl and Malinowski, among others, skepticism about African graphic systems.[60] Clearly, however, the anteriority of Egypt is established in this field as it is in every field of human science and art. Diop recognizes the primacy of Egypt in this fashion:

> L'Égypte est au reste de l'Afrique Noire ce que la Grèce et Rome sont à l'Occident. Les nouvelles humanités Africaines devront s'édifier sur les soubassements de l'antique culture pharaonique. L'égyptien ancien et le méroïtique devront remplacer le latin et le grec dans les programmes. Le droit égyptien devra prendre la place du droit romain.[61]

This profound statement places all African language systems with their various graphic systems in line for a full philosophical and linguistic relationship with the African classical cultures. Diop claims that:

> Les processus de l'évolution des langues africaines apparaît clarement; loin de nous l'idée que le walaf descende par filiation directe de l'égyptien ancien, mais le walaf, l'égyptien et les autres langues africaines dérivent d'une langue mère commune que l'on peut appeler le paleo-africain.[62]

Diop explains further that the comparison of languages, particularly at the lexical level, would permit the elimination of false etymologies. He believes that the mother language, this Diopian paleo-African language, can be shown to be common to most African languages, including ancient Egyptian. He establishes this thesis in the comprehensive and substantive *Parenté Génetique de L'Egyptien Pharaonique et des Langues Négro-Africaines* published in 1977.[63]

Unquestionably, the graphic systems of Africa, whether carved in stone, written on papyrus, formed out of objects, or shaped in the sand, represent enormous variation and complexity. In the sacred writing of ancient Egypt we see the beginning of knowledge about ourselves, about Africa, indeed, about the world because the anteriority of Egypt in graphic systems has meaning for the whole world.

African Names and Concepts as Disseminated

We find not only the origins of monumental civilization in Africa but also the linguistic basis for many Hebrew and Christian names. Moses, for example, the name of the greatest Hebrew prophet, is derived from the ancient Kemetic *msi* "to give birth," *msw* which is found in the Kemetic names *Thothmoses* "begotten of Thoth," and *Rameses* "begotten of RA." On this point it should be noted that in Yoruba the Kemetic *msi* occurs as *misi* as in *oyo misi*, the title of the kingmakers at Oyo. They are "begotten at Oyo," descendants of the soil.

Furthermore, there is some support for the view that "amen" first occurs in the pharaonic names such as Amenophis, Amenhotep, Amenomope, and Tutankhamun. Thus, the Arabic, Hebrew and Greek use of "amen" as a denouement to a praise or prayer has its base in the ancient Egyptian name for the deity, Amun. In Turkish the word "Amin" carries a meaning similar to that of "Amen" in Arabic, Hebrew, and Greek, but "Aman" is an exclamation that expresses shock and a cry for divine intervention. Both of these meanings may hark back to the ancient African deity as well. Used in Turkish to ask for forgiveness, "Aman" seeks to beg mercy from God or Allah in a desperate situation.

In view of the persistent attacks on African culture from the point of alphabetism, which is the valorization of writing as preferable to any other system of communication, it has been my intention to do two things: (1) to demonstrate that writing is not the only way to transmit culture and knowledge, and (2) to demonstrate that there is no intrinsic value in writing which constitutes a "superior" stage of evolution. The correct presentation of African graphic developments suggests that, if anything, writing began on the continent of Africa. Nevertheless, one should not assume from that position either any superiority of writing. Preiswerk and Perrot have made a valuable contribution by writing, "teaching the alphabet is obviously not ethnocentric in itself; however, the hypothesis of the universal value of literacy, conferring on it the quality of quasi-absolute objective is questionable in view of other needs of a society and its economy."[64]

I shall now turn to the discussion of the rhetorical power of Ma'at and its relationship to the practical level of human speech. Since classical African civilization in Kemet was suspended from the twin beams of literature and orature, our intellectual interest should lead to the sanguine possibilities of understanding African philosophy and language from an Afrocentric perspective rather than an anemic dismissal of the search for peace and harmony as might be the case in some European circles.

The Rhetorical Power of Ma'at

Maulana Karenga has written in *The Husia* that "Husia" signifies "the two divine powers by which Ra created the world, i.e., 'Hu,' authoritative utterance, and 'Sia,' exceptional insight."[65] Rhetoric, the theory of authoritative utterance, and oratory, elegant utterance, are intricately related to Egyptian life. In fact, despite the significance of the hieroglyphic, hieratic and demotic scripts which have given us so much information about ancient Africa, the Egyptians were primarily an oral people. The spoken word was the essential means of cultural and spiritual transmittal of values. Even the transmittal of the dead to the spirit world was accompanied by the spoken word. It is therefore no wonder that the Egyptians conceived of the concerns of oratory, the functions of rhetoric, and the nature of the systematic investigation of both the practice of public speaking, oratory, and its theory, rhetoric.

Reference to primary texts, however, provides us with our evidences since the spoken word was not preserved in ancient time. Actually, *The Coming Forth by Day* is itself a veritable expression of Egyptian style and rhetorical disposition. If we examined the canons of oratory established by the Egyptians under the tutelage of Thoth, the lord of divine speech, we will have the fundamental categories for oratory as contemporary as a Malcolm X or Martin Luther King, Jr.

For example, the origin of the introductory salutation is found in the "t'etet," oratorical expression of "adoration of Ra who rises in the eastern skies." The aim of such a salutation is to open a public speech. It was later made by the Hebrews and Arabs introductions such as "to the God of Abraham, Isaac and Jacob" or "in the name of Allah, the most merciful."

Based on the historically correct position of Africans, the introductory salutations were intended to connect the present audience to the past. The speaker, in this case, was a nexus for the past and present. In order for an orator to perform at the highest levels he had to know the special duties of the speaker which related to Ma'at. No orator could effectively speak with the eloquence of Thoth unless he understood the special character of Ma'at.

"Know thyself," the admonition written on the temple at Karnak, reverberated deep in the heart of the ancient Egyptian orator. After the union of the two kingdoms, the Egyptians attained a high degree of knowledge of their material surroundings. They had erected pyramids, carved sphinxes, graded roads, introduced geometry, studied the stars, and built beautiful temples. By 2600 B.C. the last great pyramids had been built. And yet it is not only the monumental material contributions of ancient Egypt which attract our attention. Egypt was always in search of immortality. In fact, immortality is the principle theme of its massive temples and pyramids. The quest for wisdom and truth occupied the lives of the elders but it was also a quest actively pursued by initiates who knew it as the pathway to establishing the proper order. Life was meaningless without this order. Consequently the priests as orators exercised considerable control over the philosophical thoughts of the society.

There is an account in Her-Bak that "the sage sat for a long time in silence. When Her-Bak showed uneasiness he said, 'If yesterday's lesson suggests no questions we have no starting point for today's.'" Whatever the initiate studied, nothing was so important as achieving total knowledge of self. Let me explain. The Egyptian gods gave no divine guidance. Frankfort says that the gods were known to require that a person respect Ma'at but there were no specific divine commands which shaped human action.[66] What we know is that it was considered "right" to maintain unity of heart and tongue, conviction and speech, "right" to respect authority and right to enjoy inheritance. Yet human wisdom alone gave direction, there were no directives from gods. The whole oratorical enterprise was one which followed the signposts of the sages and sought not struggle or confrontation but harmony.

On the whole, even when a person erred it was not conceived of as rebellion against god. The person did not commit a crime against god; the person was moving against the established order and the responsibility of one god or another was to see that the order was vindicated. In Egypt as throughout Africa there is no violent conflict between gods and humans; there is also no image of the individual hero. The concept "the wrath of God" does not appear either and consequently the aberrations of the Egyptians are not sinful as against god; they are the results of ignorance and the poor fellow must be disciplined. The truly ignorant knows neither good nor evil. Such a person violates the principles of Ma'at. Ignorant orators are violators of Ma'at, bringers of disharmony.

Although the book, *The Coming Forth by Day*, often called *The Book of the Dead*, deals with passage from life to death, in its deeper meaning it is a book about Ma'at. Ma'at, when applied to public speaking is the product of existential tension. A speaker achieves it only when he self-consciously knows that he is indeed alive. Ma'at, ultimately a spiritual concept, is the central notion in the questing life. Yet an orator can only become truly Ma'at-oriented in the company of a thousand gods. The one is not separated from the other, and the other cannot exist without the one. A speaker needs an audience. In fact, as Isha Schwaller de

Lubicz says, it is only "by the heart of Osiris" in us that we can become Ma'at-oriented. What is it then?

Ma'at is a social, ethical, and rhetorical term. The Egyptians understood it as the divine order of creation, of society, of nature. Since the cosmos was one they had no difficulty with Ma'at meaning justice, truth, harmony; the categories and contrasts are ours. Even today in traditional African societies medicine, ethics, and rhetoric are connected. In the West one may believe that nature is cruel and that belief does not affect anything else. This is not true in Africa. All things are connected. Among the Yoruba, a child is not a person until the name is spoken.

Ma'at becomes a symbol of the search for existential peace, it preserves whatever union with the Egyptian "deep sources" are necessary to reveal the modalities of the spirit which manifest truth, justice, and wisdom. Everything in rhetorical expression reveals unity between the person and the cosmos. This cosmos is a unified spiritual totality different from the materialized universe of a technocratic perspective which does not yield cosmos.[67] Richards is correct when she says "spirit is not separate from matter."[68] In effect, Ma'at apprehends spirit in matter. There is no oppositional element in the spiritual and material as in the western oppositions of body/mind, knowledge/opinion, male/female, science/religion, and so on. To the Egyptian the cosmos had complementary pairs. That is why the divine being in most African cultures following Egypt is androgynous, therefore able to reproduce itself. Thus, the orator searches for harmony in conflict.

The African view is little changed from this idea of unity with the cosmos. In the sense of the Zulu declaration, one says, "I am river, I am mountain, I am tree, I am love, I am emotion, I am beauty, I am lake, I am cloud, I am sun, I am sky, I am mind, I am one with one." There is no difference between human beings in-knowledge-of-themselves and the cosmos-becoming. The symbols which suggest Ma'at provide existential connections to those who would decipher the orator's message.

Ma'at's special character seems to have been righteousness and rightness in the person. Justice, truth, and righteousness were often used to denote Ma'at. Righteousness is more that the rightness we find in nature, however: righteousness is a transpersonal experience within the human order. One cannot be righteous, it is a continuous process by which we align ourselves with the harmony we find in nature. Thus, righteousness is processual and when we say "be righteous" we only mean it as a process for the moment, for the particular context. One may have integrity but one cannot have righteousness.

The orator's search for soul becomes a search for cosmic unity, better yet, cosmic union. Like the entire enterprise of the death mystery in the Egyptian pyramid narratives oratory is an effort to address the cosmic union. One merges with the past and in this merging with the past finds the pathway to the future. There is no discovery, no transpersonal insight, without according the past its proper place. This is why the most advanced psychotherapies attempt to have a person make peace with the past in a quest for present and future peace. The ancient Egyptians understood this and endeavored to ritualize the transpersonal experience by using symbolic representations of the experience. One travels as Ra travels and emerges as Ra emerges. The dead person is committed to the "womb" of the pyramid, much like the initiate is made to remain in an isolated hut, prior to receiving qualifications to enter into life. Therefore, the ancient Egyptian, as other African peoples, did not carry on a widespread practice of cremation. The aim was to have the person emerge as whole. The womb, the tomb, and the encapsulating process of searching for Ma'at in the closet of the mind as the body is secluded from the community become symbols of the quest for righteousness. The basis for oratory is found in this questing life.

Akhenaton's heresy, after thousands of years of the Egyptian attempt for harmony through Ma'at working internally, was that he sought in Aton the one cosmic generator that gave meaning to life. But this force, this one god heresy, was external, outside of the individual, a cosmic weaver weaving from afar. Thus, Akhenaton's heresy was not the elevation of Aton as the only force, nor the deemphasis of Ptah, Horus, Set, Nut, Osiris, Khnemu, or Thoth, but the replacement of the individual's quest for Ma'at with a giver or chief of Ma'at. The worship of the solar disk, solarism, reached its zenith under Akhenaton (Amenhotep IV) because he prohibited the worship of all gods except the great disk of the sun. He ordered the names of other gods erased from monuments and called Amen-Ra by the name Aton. One hymn to Amen-Ra goes "Adoration to thee, O Amen-Ra, the bull in Annu, the ruler of all the gods, the beautiful and beloved god who gives life by means of every kind of food and fine cattle." This hymn, itself rhetorical, was meant to serve rhetorical ends.

Furthermore, the priests of Thebes say, "you are chief of all the gods, lord of Ma'at, father of the gods, creator of men and women, maker of beasts and cattle, lord of all that exists .... " Ma'at becomes under the heresy a possession of Amen-Ra when before throughout the search for the transcendental state the initiate had relied upon self-consciousness produced by following a knowledge of causes. Initiates were never principal orators. They took their cues from those who possessed innate gnosis, the priests, who evoked consciousness which transcended disharmonies.

The ancient Egyptian quest for Ma'at was not linear and based on acquisition of technology but on the certitude that could only come from an understanding of causes. There again the imperative to the student "know thyself." The uncovering of the inner ear is the first requirement for being a good orator. Only through knowledge of causes can the person achieve harmony, otherwise disorder and disharmony, which represent evil, dominate. Whenever disorder exists in the individual or between the individual and nature, we have the concept of evil, the equivalent of the existentialist's indecisiveness, the only sin. In African thought, disharmony in the community must be quickly corrected. This is why there was often a dependence on the consecration made to the vital function which a particular animal incarnated. We sometimes speak of animal worship which, by the way, occurs nowhere that I know of in Africa. There are meditations, rhythmic meditations, as Robert Lawlor recognizes, that were used to clarify essential functions of nature.[69] This was not a worship of animals, but a grasping for essentiality.

The scarab, the oval, and a kneeling man with a wave over his head represent the expression "I shall come into existence." Thus spoke Ra and therein is the secret to the orator's objective. What we reach for is the source of harmony with nature, to be absorbed in the flow of the cosmos, that is the life the ancient Egyptian understood. Throughout the papyrus of Ani one finds the question, "What is it then?" The answer to this repeated question is various but in the end the message of harmony between humans and nature is clear. "I cackle as a goose, I fly as a hawk." In other words, I am one with nature. In fact if the orator's senses are trained by the laws of Ma'at, then he conforms appearance to function.

The choice of an animal as a symbol was not random. The priests did not go out and choose the first creature that came along to represent digestion but they chose the jackal. This animal kills its prey, buries it and returns to eat it when it has begun to decompose. It becomes a symbol for digestion, physical and metaphysical. We observe life, growth, death, coagulation, decomposition and transformation. No being can begin the process of rebirth until its form has disintegrated. All methods of reaching the mind understand this technically. Rhetoric is no different. The jackal-headed Anubis always led the soul of the deceased into the first stage of the dwat, world of transformations. When the body of the deceased was mummified, the organs were removed, dehydrated, and placed in urns. The urn containing the intestines has a jackal on it, suggesting the connection between the intestines and digestion. The jackal gives life through that which is poison for others. The destructive process of digestion becomes an element in transformation. As Lawlor points out, the jackal must dig up his buried morsels at the proper time or they may pass into an indigestible state of chaos.[70]

Ma'at reveals itself through the spoken word and sculpted images. A sign is often "hollowed out to signify entering into matter; it is in relief, when leaving it is signified."[71] In certain ways the tombs show this, the entry being the placing of the body into the earth; the exit being the resurrection, the rise and fall of the Nile, the ebb and flow of our existence.

Rhetoric becomes a counterweight that evaluates the heart of the living as Ma'at evaluates the dead. Ma'at is symbolized by a feather, and is present in the weighing process. A heart on a plate of balance is counterweighted by a feather representing Ma'at. The plummet or weight attached to a line represents the emotional life of a person. Ma'at has two dimensions, one is divine and the other is the individual Ma'at whom the dead should have realized in him or herself. Ma'at is cosmic consciousness, universal ideation, essential wisdom, proceeding ceaselessly from divine Ra, whose nourishment she is. A teacher is most successful when the student has a unifying vision. An orator is effective when he creates a union with his audience.

Our knowledge of the symbol is always limited. We can never know all aspects of the symbol. It is unlimited, infinite. There is no person who could know all the possibilities of a symbol. It would mean innate knowledge of the entire universe. Ma'at does not mean that, it does not imply that, but rather it suggests knowledge of self as the absolute path to knowledge of symbols. This knowledge is constructive, liberating, knowledge of synthesis as opposed to a rational, analytical knowledge which dismantles and destroys. Ma'at becomes a way to a new state of thought, a transpersonal opening of our intelligence. But this takes simplicity of heart-mind as opposed to complexity; synthesis as opposed to analysis.

Ogotemmeli, the Dogon priest, reveals to Marcel Griaule during a thirty-day interview that the Dogon people of Mali know that the time has come when secret things must be said. The Dogon knew that intuitive sensations held the mysterious call to knowledge. Spirit-energy, soul dominates matter and matter may be a temporary phenomenon anyway, particularly in its relationship to life. When the body is dead, life is thought to be transcendental to matter and independent of the physical and chemical laws that govern matter. The Egyptians did not put it just that way but they understood that Ma'at, the ultimate cause, did not operate wholly within the framework of material laws. The images, symbols, found in the temples and tombs were only representative of the innate knowledge and absolute truth that existed apart from the material.

There is a verse in the Ifa divination of the Yoruba which reads "ologbon kan o ta koko omi seti aso" or "no wise person can tie water into a knot." Ma'at is like this. It is not subject to the whims of outside forces, it exists within a person. We must find it in ourselves, flowing forward harmoniously. This is the lesson of the ancient Egyptians.

Interdependence and reciprocity, according to Richards, are seen in ritual sacrifice.[19] As the ultimate philosophic expression, ritual serves to provide symbolic truth to our relationship with

Ma'at. We die and are reborn through symbols and the light as a feather symbol of Ma'at, the judge of our heart, revitalizes us. Rhetoric is preeminently theory about the use of symbols.

The African American knows "this little light of mine" shines because of Ma'at. We are eternally being born in the affirmation of life. As testaments to the abiding influence of the ancient Egyptians we celebrate the affirmation of a judgment rendered in our favor. Ma'at judgment validates our inner work for harmony and humanness.

Let us understand. The cause is seen through the effect. Observation of a concrete symbol of a fact helps to evoke its abstraction. Throughout the Egyptian myth there is a knowledge of the successive appearance of divine properties which have emerged from the original unity where these properties are in a latent state—then there is a knowledge of these properties in the continuous creation where they are made known by nature. It is possible to speak of the neters, gods of Egypt, as a "hierarchy of the neters" much like in the later Hindu or Hebrew Cabbala, but in one important way this hierarchy of the gods is unlike those traditions—it is not "dogmatized." The neters do not have a hierarchy based on their appearance as primary or secondary causes and do not have a hierarchy based on the nature of their function, spiritual, or material. The Egyptians, like other Africans, have scattered the elements of knowledge, and one has to fit them together like a puzzle in order to know the picture.

Ma'at is the cumulative appearances of the divine properties. I smell a flower and say "wonderful." I am surely at that moment full of wonder. A myriad of experience, all connected to the latent unity, work the miracle of Ma'at for us as we either speak or hear spoken the golden words of Thoth. There is something which transcends myth; Ma'at is truth in all things, the reason of life, the purpose of speech, and the source of happiness. Nature itself gives us the concrete meanings to abstractions; it reveals symbolic forms and expressions that may be spoken. That is why no access to the "keys" of this knowledge will help us unless we adopt our way of seeing to the simplicity of synthesis.

There are few African myths of the universe emerging out of chaos. Harmony preexists chaos, it comes before confusion and turmoil, and is in itself, in the African view, the original condition. Whether you study the ancient Kemetic view or the various derivatives of that view you find that harmony is at the center of existence. The Yoruba claim that it was after Orunmila had done his great works that his children on earth brought about confusion. Yoruba is only one of the great traditions that emphasizes the concept of harmony out of which the world began.

Ma'at functions as the celebration of harmony and balance in the life of African people. While I may refer to various myths from African history, it is important that we do not confuse myths with theologies, philosophies, or ideologies. Myths are tales. They are not meant to provide a systematic treatment of theology, philosophy, or ideology, but they give us explanations of origins in the form of tales. Therefore I shall use the ancient Kemetic conception of Ma'at as a point of departure in a discussion of the African way against injustice. But those are analyses developed with the idea of bringing to the fore a fundamental idea rooted in African culture. What a systematic account, such as I propose here, will do is to demonstrate organic connectives to African culture in continental and diasporan African areas. In pursuit of this connective I shall examine, first and in brief outline, the idea of Ma'at in Kemet, Ma'at in African commonalities, and the transformation of Ma'atic ideas in the diaspora. Certainly I recognize that this in and of itself is not enough in methodological terms, so I endeavor to establish a methodological direction, that is, how do Afrocentrists arrive at a Ma'atic condition in contemporary society.

Ma'at is sometimes called the Kemetic quality of "order," "justice," "righteousness," and "balance." Each of these terms is important in understanding the concept, yet neither one is sufficient in and of itself. Ma'at is a vast ocean and there are many waves that constitute its meaning. Indeed Ma'at may be seen as a cosmic element similar in its energy to Asé in Yoruba. Eshu is able to maintain balance and order in society by the use of Axé. We are correct if we see Ma'at as the ruling force between good and evil. When you speak of it as the organizing principle of human society, the creative spirit of phenomena, and the eternal order of the universe, you come close to understanding what the ancient Kemetic civilization understood.

The permutations of the Kemetic concept may be found in numerous other cultures. For example, the Old English word for measure is "Maeth," the Dutch word for measure is "Maat" and the Amharic word for balance is "Meezan." Furthermore, the West African language of Hausa use the expression "Ma'aunu" for measuring scales. The word "mathematics" finds its source in the ancient Kemetic Ma'at through the Greek "Mathematikos" and the Latin "Mathematicus." Both the Greek and the Latin words use the ancient stem "Mathe" which carries the meaning of precision and exactness. In this sense they are related to the Kemetic idea of measure. Lacking an imperialistic ethos, Kemet did not spread its concepts by force of arms like Rome or Islam but by the truth of its ideal.

This idea of Ma'at is the idea of justice not merely in legal terms but in terms of the proper relationship between a human person and the universe, between the person and nature, between the person and another person. Thus, Ma'at means that which is perfectly established, fixed in the position of good because it possesses the quality of a force, energy which regulates the relationship of the universe. So the kings of Egypt were not merely kings, they were the embodiment of the concept of Ma'at, and the goddess Ma'at stood with them so long as they stood with Ma'at. They did not have empirical testing and quantification of the type often thought of today; they had evidence of the truth in the proper relationship of things, in the propriety of human beings to the order maintained by the gods.

Therefore, our understanding of Ma'at in the Kemetic tradition is predicated on our appreciation for the concept of order, measure, limit, and form, that is, form in the sense of order and justice. Ma'at confirmed the stability of society and nature. If one looks at the later Greek derivations, we see that the Greeks took the Kemetic traditions and misunderstood them. George James, in *Stolen Legacy*, tells us that there is no Greek philosophy, only stolen African philosophy.

The Greeks, particularly Pythagoras and Heraclitus, took the Kemetic idea of Ma'at and attempted to change it into mathematics. Aristotle says that the followers of Pythagoras devoted themselves to mathematics as if it constituted the only form. They said that things consisted of numbers. Many descendants of Pythagoras still believe this strange doctrine. It should be pointed out, however, that Pythagoras came to this view for religious reasons.

Affected by the Kemetic teachings on the immortality of the soul, Pythagoras sought to utilize as much of the priestly teachings of Kemet as he could in the development of his own views. He reached into Africa for some sense of reality since the Homeric gods were not real gods as far as he was concerned. They were just like human beings. He wanted something that was different, perhaps distant, more distant than the Homeric gods. They could neither inspire others nor be the objects of worship. The religion of Dionysus, borrowed from ancient Kemet, had satisfied some of the Greek yearning for transcendence in the seventh century B.C. but this was a caricature of Kemetic religion. The Dionysians often worked themselves into a frenzy and exhausted themselves drinking animal blood.

Pythagoras rebelled against this as pagan and introduced the idea of a spectator who sits back and observes life. Thus, the Greek word "theory" means also to "look on." I think that Pythagoras' idea of form by which he meant "limit" in a numerical sense was an attempt to re-recreate the Kemetic Ma'at in secular terms. For Pythagoras, for example, harmony in the form that the limiting structure of numerical ratio imposes upon the unlimited possibilities for sounds, say, with the strings of a musical instrument. In medicine he saw the same principle at work. Health was the harmony or balance or proper ratio of certain opposites such as hot and cold, wet and dry, and various other elements. But these concepts are found in the Kemetic idea that health is only possible when the body is "in tune" with nature. In every African society the same principle adheres. The difference is that the Greeks wanted to quantify this—how many, how much.

Heraclitus introduced to the Greeks the terms flux and unity. All things were in flux and therefore you cannot step in the same river twice. Things are forever changing. This idea of flux is applied to everything, including the soul. Thus in the sixth century B.C. Heraclitus was grappling with the concept of balance by introducing the idea of flux. But this was a particularistic notion, not holistic, and very much like Anaximenes' notion that air was the key to everything because it was everywhere. One day the Greeks thought the key was air, the next day they said it was fire, then they said it was earth or water, when in fact the Kemetians recognized that there were all interactive concepts. They operated in relationship to each other.

Throughout the history of Kemet, even when Tuthmosis III bestrode the world as the favorite son of Hatshepsut, and down to the reigns of Pianki and Tarharka, the idea of order and justice was incorporated in the total relationship of the Universe, all things were connected. Ma'at encapsulated the idea of rightness. In fact, Tuthmosis III's instructions to his vizier Rekhmire were etched into the wall of Rekhmire's tomb. In the wall paintings Ma'at was personified as Ma'at, the goddess; Ma'at was the feather balanced against the heart of a dead person to check that the candidates for entry to heaven could truly claim to be free of evil; Ma'at stood in judgment as a living goddess; Ma'at was a proper behavior towards others, towards nature; Ma'at was a pragmatic approach to moral or ethical life. In the words of Tuthmosis III, "Look to the office of vizier. It sustains the lands. When a petitioner comes from Upper or Lower Kemet see that everything done conforms to the spirit of the law. A petitioner should not say, 'My right has been denied me.' The god hates partiality; treat the person you know equally with the person you do not. Let men respect you because you offer justice. This is laid upon you."

Ma'at in African Commonalities

A fundamental position of my argument is that all African societies find Kemet a common source for intellectual and philosophical ideas. These manifestations are shown, for example, in: the conversations of the Dogon's blind philosopher Ogotommeli; Zulu oral poetry, as brought to us by Masizi Kunene; Yoruba Ifa divination rights; Nsibidi texts, and in the practices and words of the Shona spirit mediums. Wole Soyinka has argued that African culture is one and that the idea of a unity of African culture is not to be looked upon as retrogressive.[73] This is the position I take with respect to the dissemination of the Ma'atic concept throughout the African world.

There are five Kemetic concepts that constitute the Ma'atic response to injustice and disorder in the world. Those concepts must be seen in the light of general African cultural developments. You cannot separate Kemet from an understanding of the basic ideas in Baganda and Kikuyu or Dinka. For this reason I have gone to the idea of Ma'at in search of its manifestations in the Kemetic tradition and have tried to see how those traditions appear in other parts of the African world. Certainly there are differentials in response based upon environmental conditions and other factors but I believe that the general cultural project against chaos represented by Ma'at with an ankh in her hand is encompassed by my classification, using five Kemetic concepts: tep, pet, heb, sen, and meh.

Tep (Beginning)

> Love of Children
> Late Weaning
> Age-grouping
> Value Fertility

Pet (Extensions)

> Society above Individual
> Extended Family
> Honor to Ancestors

Heb (Festival)

> Agricultural Rites
> Art for Ritual
> Dance/Music
> Gift-Giving
> Ceremony for Passages
> Ululations

Sen (Circle)

> Burial
> Extended Funeral
> Living Ancestors

Meh (Crowning Glory)
> Supreme Deity
> Search for Harmony (Ma'at)
> Freedom from Shame

The transformation of these concepts throughout Africa and the African world has meant that the influence of Kemet continues unabated even in the language and behavior of African Americans. We are essentially a people of Ma'at, we cannot escape it because it is based upon thousands of years of history. C. Tsehloane Keto tells the story of a European missionary who had great difficulty with a man in southern Africa whom he was trying to convert. He asked the man if he had sinned, the man being more than sixty-five years old. The African responded to the European that he had not sinned. Confused, the European said, you cannot live so long without sinning, it is not possible. Therein is the problem the African may have committed many acts that the European may have called sins but in the Ma'atic formulation whenever he had done so he had corrected the balance, he had performed the rituals that would have restored the balance. Therefore, he had not sinned in his tradition or in the Europeans because the right ordering of relationships, the performance of the necessary rites re-establishes the justness of the society.

Among the Sotho and the Xhosa all order begins with human beings existing in a state of order internally and externally. The proper kind of relationship to the universe is one of balance, rhythm, circularity, and justness. The idea of evil resides in the ability of a person to "mess around with" the natural order, to tamper with the state of harmony. But evil is always associated with human beings; it does not, and cannot exist apart from some human touch. Once evil is found to be present and human beings appear to be in a state of confusion because of it, then there has to be a ritual to make it right, to rebalance the natural order. The Ma'atic force is always greater than evil force.

Almost every human activity that involves a negative action that causes the balance to be lost must be dealt with through some form of cleansing. If a person accidentally kills someone that person must be cleansed. Purification is essential to the restoration of balance. Armies that go into battle and struggle with opposing armies must have purification ceremonies before and after battle. War is the epitome of society in turmoil. Cleansing is essential for soldiers. Thus, even in contemporary times, such as with the struggle for Zimbabwe, the soldiers were cleansed by the spirit medium Nehanda before they went into battle. All of this is related to balance. It cannot be escaped that wholeness, integrity, security, and justice are related to the idea of restoring harmony.

Ma'at is the fundamental reality, without it there is no under-standing, no harmony, and no possible restoration of balance. We are isolated satellites without power or direction drifting into space. Ma'at imposes order and direction, gives us a true and adequate meaning of our life and is the major force against chaos. God does not hold the world on his shoulders as the Greeks believed but she, as the goddess Ma'at kept the universe from the disorder. The king, though a god, could not rule arbitrarily. Like all things in the universe he was subject to Ma'at.

Ma'at was the incantation of truth and justice, but more than that because it was the cosmic principle of harmony. But Africans have continued to say that you cannot have harmony without truth and justice.

The Kemetic idea was to represent Ma'at as a charming figure, wearing an ostrich plume on her head and often holding an ankh. The vizier, the Supreme Judge of Kemet, was the Priest of Ma'at. He served her primary interest in keeping chaos from entering the sanctuary of order. Nothing was more important than putting truth in the place of falsity, maintaining harmony's strength over conflict, and righting wrong in the nature of things. Everything was affected. If a vase was on its side, you righted it; if a staff fell to the ground from its position against the wall, you stood it up again. Thus, every act of protocol was connected to Ma'at; all decency, courte-sies, and habits of cleanliness were related to Ma'at. This diminu-tive figure of Ma'at represented the concept of Ma'at as all-inclu-sive and all-forceful, that is, in the language of force. The original force field was the concept of Ma'at. Amenhotep III put the conviction of the kings best when he said that his whole aim was to make Kemet blossom as it had in "primeval times" by means of Ma'at. This is a powerful statement of purpose.

The cosmos regulated all of its parts and these parts were organic to each other. In their relationship they constituted a perfect order. Included in this perfection was the human being, the heavenly bodies, the change of seasons, the rising and setting of the sun, the yearly overflowing of the Nile, and the maintenance of a stable society. When a king was Ma'atic, the people were secure, and their trust in their government was assured. Security, therefore, in life and death, in social order and cosmic order, was reaffirmed forever from the moment of creation by the enactment of ritual.

There is both continuity and circularity in this idea of Ma'at. The principle of eternal recurrence is central to the Kemetic world-view. That is why it is impossible to separate the beginning from the crowning glory but rather to see them as constant re-enactments of the truth of order. We help to hold the world together through ritual observance. Ultimately that is what we are doing when we turn a behavior into a rite. The Eurocentric idea of straightforward progression in time from beginning to end did not occur in Kemetic thought. African thought was in terms of cycles, circles, continuity. When a king took the throne, he reaffirmed Ma'at. His ascension signified that he returned to the everlasting beginnings of the cosmic order and thus kept it going by his divinity. It is this circularity that is at the heart of the concept of kingship in all African societies. One may easily confuse the Eurocentric idea of the divine rights with the African idea of the king as expressive of Ma'atic continuity. One leads to formulations like that expressed by the caesars, the emperors, or the Russian czars, in which a person can claim to be anything he wants to be. This is a very individualistic concept. Different czars possessed different attitudes toward their duties and offices and had different directions in their reigns, but the Kemetic ruler was in fact the embodiment of something eternal, something superior to the hold of the office. This is the relationship of the Oba, the Alafin, and the king of Baganda to reality; this is an underlying commonality in African societies.

A Search for Method

The search for method has now been joined in earnest by several Afrocentric scholars. The task for method, however, is enormous because it must admit an approach which takes into consideration many African cultures, the dissemination of Kemetic ideas, and the closeting of certain rituals behind esoteric ceremonies as the priests responded to foreign encroachments. None of this is impossible. But as the Akan say, "the person who can untie this knot knows the secret of the dja."

Niangoran-Bouah's book, *The Akan World of Gold Weights* is a most valuable advance in our approach to Ma'at.[74] The whole idea of dja is close to Ma'at. The dja is not merely gold-weights but the Akan concept of order, balance, fairness, justice. Niangoran-Bouah says the dja dates back to the beginning of time. While all elements of the dja, figurative and geometrical, are weights, they represent the sacred, special place of the idea in African society. The word adja, heritage, for example, comes from the word dja. The dja being passed on to a relative at death. But dja is a concept, a philosophical concept that goes beyond the mere idea of weights; it is a Ma'atic concept with the aspects of balance, justice, fairness, and integrity playing a major role in our understanding of it. One is not just dealing with gold-weights when one discusses dja; one is also encountering Ma'at in its Akan manifestation.

What is true of Akan is also true of Yoruba. Ifa, or Orunmila, is the spirit of divination among the Yoruba, but that is not the end of Ifa. The priest of Ifa, the Babalawo, is the one who has the secret. What is the secret that is held by Babalawo? It is the esoteric knowledge through which he can open the future and learn the wish of Ifa. Thus when a child is born, when a marriage is proposed, when laying the foundations of a town, or when making war or making peace, one consults with Ifa. The reason this is so is because Ifa is Ma'atic, that is, Ifa serves to reestablish the balances that have been destroyed or to prevent the harmony from descending into conflict. One cannot believe in Ma'at and not understand that Ifa comes from the same source. Ancient Kemet stands to Yoruba, Akan, Shona, and African Americans like the step pyramid of Zoser stands in relationship to all other pyramids, first and prototypical. This is the basic philosophical perspective on method.

There are four elementary considerations in the attempt to establish a method for assuring the ascendancy of Ma'at:

1. The Unity of Occasion/Situation
2. The Elimination of Chaos
3. The Elevation of Peace among Disparate Voices
4. The Creation of Harmony and Balance

Any text or person in action may be examined from these elementary considerations. The establishment of Ma'at and the Ma'atic principles, which now we can claim to be not a world view but more correctly a world voice, rests upon these four columns of analysis.

A person who seeks the road to Ma'at must come by the column of unity. This, of course, is no miracle because consciousness precedes unity. The person who wants to analyze anything for the purpose of synthesis will find that the first rule is to examine the object, thing, person, speech for unity. As Afrocentricists, that is our first obligation because it is the first step on the road to Ma'at.

If a person, object, thing, or book seek to eliminate chaos, that is also on the path to Ma'at. We tell by the thematic choice, the treatment of that choice, and the resolution of a problem whether the elimination for chaos was important for the person or not.

Peace is not the absence of struggle. In truth sometimes peace is only found in struggle. But the elevation of peace, predicated on justice and fairness, can be identified as Ma'atic. You can examine any person or occasion for the qualities of peace. There are always people who misunderstand peace-loving for weakness, but the Ma'atic world voice shows the search for peace to be one way to tell if a person or document is on the proper pathway.

Harmony is the final stage of Ma'at; it is the African way against injustice and chaos. We arrive at it through the integrity of ideas, without shame, and of course, without guilt since guilt is unknown in traditional African culture. Shame is the moral enforcer in African culture; guilt is a European individualistic concept.

Churchward's Signs and Symbols

Several nineteenth and twentieth century European writers thought to place Africa in its anterior place by writing meaningful, though sometimes flawed, accounts of African origin.

Albert Churchward's massive work on *The Signs and Symbols of Primordial Man*, first published in 1913, came as a shock to the keepers of what Martin Bernal calls the Aryan model. There were several major contributions presented by Churchward: (1) the African origin of signs and symbols, (2) the diffusion of African symbolism to the Pacific and Central America, and (3) the debt freemasonry owed to Africans.

The work of Churchward was in the tradition of the researches of Gerald Massey, Leo Wiener, and other Egyptologists. In his response to critics he maintained that all signs and symbols origi- nated from the African's stellar, lunar, and solar mythos. Indeed, the original Australians were part of the African exodus.[75] Church- ward argues that the Egyptian *Book of the Dead* is the key of the door and without it one cannot "trace back the history of this world—the history of all religions, and the history of all mankind, and that which is attached thereto."[76] Furthermore, Churchward says that:

... the first or Paleolithic man was the Pygmy, who was evolved in Central Africa at the sources of the Nile, or Nile valley, and that from here all originated and were carried throughout the world, and that the most primitive phase of mythology is a mode of representing certain elemental powers by means of living types which were superhuman, like the natural phenomena. The foundations of mythology were laid in the preanthropomorphic shape of primitive representation. Thus the typical giant, Apap, was an enor- mous water reptile. The typical genetrix and mother of life was a Water Cow, that represented the earth; the typical provider was a goose, etc. It was here, in the Nile valley, that the dumb mythology became articulate. Egypt alone preserved primitive gnosis and gave expression to the language of signs and symbols, and it was here that the first elemental powers were divinised, here that Totemism, Stellar, Lunar and Solar Mythology originated.[77]

What is remarkable in Churchward's work is the fact that he argued that Africa was the origin of the human race fifty years before Leakey's fossil discoveries in East Africa.

> We say that the human race originated, or was planted, in the northeast of Africa (including the sources and the banks of the Nile), and it is a very important fact to note here that the symbology has been carried down amongst ourselves to the present day.[78]

Although Churchward's interest was on the rise of freemasonry, he demonstrated in his extensive research the African origin of signs and symbols from the stellar, lunar and solar mythos. Unquestionably, Churchward was a Eurocentrist, writing as a European, and so many of his references and descriptions contain language from the racist context of his day, e.g., "pygmy," "negro." Nevertheless, his observations and insights are valuable in the realm of research open to all methods of inquiry.

Churchward was not the first and would not be the last European scholar to shake the foundations of the intellectual constructions built to deny Africa its anterior place in human civilization. In a recent book, Bernal has discussed the African impact on Greek culture by examining the role Egypt played in the development of Athenian ideas and culture. Egypt became known among Greeks soon after Homer's visit to Africa. Greeks found great fascination with early African civilization and incorporated much of African culture into their society.

Aigyptos from the original H-ka-pth, "House of the spirit of Ptah," is usually given as the general name for Egypt but was only used initially by the Greeks in reference to the lower part of Egypt. Most of Egypt had been referred to as Kemet by its inhabitants from time immemorial.

Kemet and Greek Culture

Since Egypt preceded the civilizations of Greece and Rome in antiquity it is only natural that it would be the source of much Greek knowledge, even names of towns and deities. In fact Bernal argues that

both the city name Athenai and the divine name Athene or
Athena derive from the Egyptian Ht Nt. In antiquity,
Athena was consistently identified with the Egyptian
goddess Nt or Neit. Both were virgin divinities of warfare,
weaving and wisdom. The cult of Neit was centred on the
city of Sais in the Western Delta, whose citizens felt a
special affinity with the Athenians. Sais was a secular
name, the city's religious title being Ht Nt (Temple or
House of Neit). This name is not attested in Greek or
Coptic, but the toponymic element Ht- is transcribed as
At- or Ath-. It was also extremely common for Egyptian
words to have what are called prothetic vowels before the
first consonant. In this case the likelihood that Nt was
preceded by a vowel is increased by the name Anat, given
to a very similar West Semitic goddess; hence it would
seem legitimate to propose a vocalization of *At(h)anait
for Ht Nt. The lack of i in Athene, Athana in the Doric
dialect and A-ta-na in Linear B would seem to be a problem. However, Attic and Doric have the variants Athenaia
and Athanaia, while the full Homeric form is Athenaie.
And as final -ts were dropped in both Greek and Late
Egyptian, the letter's non-appearance in Athenai and
Athene should be expected.[79]

Thus, there is strong evidence that the name of Greece's principal
city is nothing more than a name given by the Egyptians or taken
from the Egyptian city of Sais. Indeed, Bernal continues with his
argument in this fashion:

If the phonetic fit is good, the semantic one is perfect.
As I have said, the Ancients saw Neit and Athena as two
names for the same deity. In Egypt it was normal for a
divinity to be addressed by the name of her or his dwel-
ling, and this would explain the Greek confusion between
the names of the goddess and her city. Finally there is the
statement, by Charax of Pergamon in the second century
A.D., that "the Saitians called their city Athenai," which
makes sense only if they Ht Nt as a name for Sais.[80]

A method of historical or cultural analysis centered on African data must deal with the relationship of Africa to Europe generally and in antiquity Egypt to Greece particularly. The reason this is important is to establish for Africans in the Americas and in Africa the organic nature of the contribution of the Black world to the civilizing of Europe. Bernal says,

> Sais was on the frontier of Egypt and Libya and was sometimes part Libyan, which explains Herodotos' detailed description of Athena's association with Libya; it is also clear that this first great Greek historian thought the Egyptians and some Libyans were black.[81]

If evidence suggests that Africa was the mother of European civilization, what force brought about the demise of respect for Africa? Greece gained in prominence while Egypt fell in reputation due to a combination of European racism and chauvinism. Africa's antiquity was no longer considered a valuable credit but rather a debit.

Some writers have shown that the intensity of northern European racism was different and new. In fact, before the sixteenth century dark skin was often glorified by whites. Racism grew with the European "voyages of discovery" where adventurers came into contact with diverse peoples. But it had existed in the early writings of Aristotle who saw the Greeks as superior to other people, particularly those who lived in cold regions of Europe and who, he believed, had courage but no brainpower and Asiatics who he said had brains but no courage. Racial superiority existed in Aristotle as it was to later exist in John Locke, David Hume, Voltaire, and Thomas Jefferson. In fact, as Bernal has shown, David Hume and Benjamin Franklin linked dark skin to moral and mental inferiority.[82]

Chief among the views that increased the decline of Egypt in the minds of Europeans was the idea of polygenesis and geographic determinism. Both concepts are parts of the same cultural approach to race. Jean Bodin, Montesquieu and Rousseau all participated, from the French side, in this establishment of European superiority based on geography and topography. Of course, Aristotle placed

Greece in the favorite position. Montesquieu's racism fully blossomed in his *Spirit of Laws* published in 1748 while Rousseau's *Social Contract* published in 1762 argued that Europe was the best repository of human achievement. Bernal has argued that the idea of progress and romanticism also assisted in the supplanting of Egypt and the rise of Greece. There is a clear changeover in the thinking of the Europeans from the fourteenth and fifteenth centuries. The impact of the translation into Italian of *Hieroglyphika*, a fifth century work by Horapollo, an Egyptian, was felt throughout Europe. This was almost the culmination of the early appreciation of Egypt by Europe.

By the beginning of the fifteenth century, Italian scholars had a good idea of the centrality of Egypt and the Hermetic Texts to the ancient learning they wished to revive. Scholars had long known about and read *Asclepius*, and Arabic Hermetic Texts were being translated into Latin. Furthermore, with the increase in contact between Italy and Greece the Neo-Platonic and Hermetic writings of Psellos and the other promoters of the Byzantine Renaissance became available.[83]

Our method, to be exact, must reconstruct the place of ancient Egypt in order to adequately deal with the history of Africa. In fact, the Europeans, particularly the Italians during the so-called Renaissance (it was a renaissance because of the primacy of Egypt) adopted Egyptian knowledge as the basis of their own.

The Renaissance passion for Egypt came firstly from its ancient reputation of having been the place where the mysteries and sacred initiations were first established. Furthermore, with the possible exceptions of the Persian Zoroastrians and the Chaldaeans, of whom there was only a dim conception, the Egyptians were seen as the origin of all wisdom and arts; for all the sense of progress attributed to them by Romantic historians, Renaissance men and women were fundamentally interested in the past. They were searching for *fontes* or "sources"—and so they

looked behind Christianity to pagan Rome, behind Rome
to Greece; but behind Greece there was Egypt.... [84]

Egypt was the remarkable ideal, the purest symbol of antiquity, and
the civilization most worthy of emulation. In fact, the demand by
Cosimo de Medici in 1460 that the *Corpus Hermeticum* of Hermes
Trismegistos be translated into Italian before Plato's *Republic* or
Symposium was due to the belief that Egypt was before Greece, the
Corpus Hermeticum before the *Republic* and Hermes before Plato.
Marsilio Ficino, the Florentine scholar and translator, used the
Corpus Hermeticum as the foundation for the Platonic Academy.
Indeed, Plato's own Athenian academy had its foundation in the
Egyptian models. Bernal believes that the election of new members
in European academies is a practice, with its paraphernalia and
ceremonies, derived from the Egyptian sacred initiation rites.[85] We
can now trace the graduation exercise in Western schools and
universities back to the temples of Egypt. Plato's own initiation at
Sais is directly linked backward to centuries of Egyptian practices
and forward to the European experience. In almost every compartment of European life they found Egypt as every door. If they
sought the gods through Mercury, Jupiter, Mars, or later in
Germanic lands in Odin, Thor or Ty, they found Osiris, Horus,
Ptah, Amen. Scarabs, serapis, and bulls with solar discs on their
foreheads and statues of lions appear throughout Europe. Childaric,
the father of Clovis who was France's first Christian king, was
buried with scarabs and the head of a bull with a solar disc on his
forehead in 481 A.D.

The Question of Proof

Two historical developments sustained the legitimacy of human
institutions for Europeans. Neither occurred in the North American
continent nor in this century, yet they have legitimized the procedure employed by institutions in the American society and are
particularly relevant where intellectual method is preserved. Both
developments relate to the concept of proof. Originally perceived
in relationship to public discourse in ancient Egypt, Sicily and
Greece, proof was a rhetorical idea meant to serve the interest of
persuasion. The first development was in the area of how proof

was secured. Those who effectively used the constituents of proof secured adherence to their positions. Logos, Pathos, and Ethos were the pillars of proof the Greeks inherited from Africa. Priestly training in Kemet had emphasized skills in rational explanation, the proper use of emotions and the character of the priest. A person who combined these traits could prove to be a wise priest. Aristotle who first wrote these proofs in Greek said that logos referred to logical appeals, pathos to emotional appeals, and ethos to character appeals. In Kemet, Imhotep is the most representative figure of this movement, although Pepi must be considered significant. The renunciation of these "pagan" ideas of proof and the institutionalization of Western notions of proof during the European Middle Ages constituted a major development in authoritative discussion. The influence of the barbarians was widespread. Entry of the Germanic tribes, Visigoths, Ostrogoths, and Vandals into the remnants of the Roman Empire and the Holy Roman Empire pressured the existing Christian pedagogical system inherited from the pagan Romans to adopt new concepts of proof. The Holy Roman Church, eager to extend its influence, bent to the demands of its new adherents who brought with them an extensive system of proof derived from their history. The Germans introduced oaths, ordeals and duels as the triune divinities of proof and in the process dethroned the pre-Christian ideas logos, pathos, and ethos. The Church acquiesced and permitted priests to serve as mediators, judges and officials in matters of proof. With the institutionalization of this trinity a person who was accused of a crime had the burden of proving himself innocent by one of the legitimate proofs: oath, ordeal or duel. No longer was it sufficient for a person to use mere logic, emotion, and character in a defense, he must demonstrate his innocence by successfully going through the trials. This concept of proof so enthusiastically adopted by the church was an attempt to delimit and conquer the pagan German gods by allowing the Christian God to assume the burden of protecting the innocent. Thus when one chose to prove his innocence what he was saying in effect was that God would allow him to pass the trial because a good God could not punish an innocent person. Many innocent persons lost their lives in a show of their righteousness.

Oaths required witnesses to the degree of the crime's severity and the accused social status. All accused persons could choose compurgators to bear witness to their oath-taking. If the accused should stumble or slip or forget the words of the oath, he was judged guilty. An innocent person would speak the words of the oath flawlessly. Ordeals were physical tests involving only the accused and usually were tests in extreme hot or cold. A person would be required to retrieve a pebble from a container of boiling water. If the hand manifested any type of burn the accused was adjudged guilty as charged. Sometimes the ordeal would require the accused to be tied with a rope and dropped in a body of water. If he sank, he was innocent; on the other hand, floaters were truly guilty because the nature of water, being purified by the priest and thereby holy, refused to receive a guilty, and therefore evil body into itself. How many innocent persons who were tried by this proof lived to celebrate their innocence is hard to say. Duels required the accused and the accuser to engage in a physical contest against each other. Again the idea was the inevitability of innocence being protected by God.

When Pope Innocent called the Fourth Lateran Council in 1215 he explicitly forbade priests to officiate at ordeals and duels. Proof of guilt or innocence was to be discovered in the proper application of the scriptures. Only the priests in England obeyed, probably at the behest of King John who owed Innocent a favor for his declaration annulling the Magna Carta. Three years later, however, when both John and Innocent were dead, the Magna Carta was reinstated by the English barons. Throughout the Holy Roman Empire the decline in Western European influences was felt as the church imposed Christian culture with its Hebraic-Greco-Roman ethos over the whole of Europe. Nevertheless, by this time the impact of the flirtation with competitive and combative proofs had left an indelible imprint on Western notions of legitimacy.

The second historical development which assisted the sustenance of legitimacy of institutions is the publication of Bishop Richard Whatley's *Elements of Logic* and *Essentials of Rhetoric*, 1826 and 1828 respectively. Whatley spent a lifetime defending Christian evidences. From his belief that the proof of God needed no demonstration but that the disproof of God's existence needed demonstration, he evolved the doctrines of presumption and burden of proof. Perhaps no two notions have aided and abetted the maintenance of the status quo and the sustenance of institutional legitimacy than presumption and burden of proof.

Presumption is the preoccupation of the ground. Something is presumed to be true unless arguments are adduced against it. The burden of proof rests with the person who would move the presumption. Changing the presumption from existing institutions has become increasingly more difficult as institutions have acquired new techniques for managing public impressions. Rather than operate as mere institutions pre-occupying ground and thus establishing their legitimacy and presumption, the institutions have gone on the offensive with the best traditions of oaths, ordeals, and duels. They present themselves as the best possible institutions to do what they do and that there are no reasonable alternatives to be chosen. Defiance of the public coupled with invitation to challenge has become a common occurrence as institutions of power, whether academic or political, rest on their acquired positions.

⌈A proper attitude toward human discovery and human knowledge depends on views that do not cast aside others' ways of knowing as unimportant. Indeed, any appropriate history cannot see some as in history and others as out of history. In this regard culture becomes more significant than civilizations as basis for moving toward universal respect and appreciation. For the Africalogist, method must always possess Afrocentric place but not exclusive territory on phenomena. I speak of this type of method as a motive of Africalogical research, the soul of method.⌋

It is necessary to examine what is meant by the soul of method. I shall deal here with the meaning of soul as a concrete motive, in the sense of activator, in Afrocentric research. Soul is the vitality the researcher brings to the Afrocentric method, that is, the creative energy used to effect a successful project. The concept is similar to Wade Nobles' idea of cultural substance which he sees as the "ontological principle of consubstantiation."[86] But I mean something more than an ontological principle when I say soul of method. This is not a mere oxymoron but what the Yoruba often call Asè, the force itself. Perhaps the only appropriate analogy to this concept of the soul of method is the vital genesis of form in African art where every art object acquires power as soon as it is consecrated in a particular way. Comments by a number of scholars underscore my observation in this regard. Ho:ton has written of the Kalabari people that "it is men who make the gods important," and further "the forehead of the spirit ... implies not just something which is intimately linked to a spirit, but something which exercises a kind of control over it."[87] Similarly, as Asè exercises control over objects, soul exercises a guiding light over method. The indwelling vital energy must be present in the scholar's work for it to be successful. There is nothing mysterious in this type of appreciation of the human process of activating Afrocentric research. Indeed, the human personality keeps the Asè active and vital. In research, the scholar must understand that everything is potentially active, powerful, and possible and it is up to the scholar to access the vitality of a project. This is different from any transmutation of matter into spirit as the European artist might reluctantly concede but rather spirit resides in matter by virtue of the universality of vital forces in objects. Thus, the soul of method responds not to clenched forms for the benefit of some judgmental audience but to matter itself as represented in the carrying out of the method. In a fundamental way this approach differs from the European emphasis on prediction and individuality. Denis Williams observed several years ago in regards to artistic practice how African systems differed from European systems of art:

> This difference between the two artistic systems, African and European, is reflected in the relative standpoints of the artist in the separate cultures. Where the practice of art for the European is individualistic and autobiographical, for the African it is anonymous and social.[88]

Williams recognizes in the field of art what the Africalogists must understand when approaching a research project. Soul, as a concrete motive force, activates research by engaging the researcher in a effort to explain human functioning by relating to concrete human conditions and cultural factors.[89]

African history and culture, as I have demonstrated, find their source and origin in the primacy of Africa in the development of human society. In addition, its zenith in antiquity was manifest in the Nile Valley Civilizations. There, the double-crown represented a union of regions, upper and lower Egypt, and the Per-Ab was the lord of the two lands. Hence, almost from the beginning the history and the mythology of Africa are based on union. To wear the two crowns, the red and the white was to announce that conflict was symbolically overcome by joining the two parts. It is this history of acceptance, this adaptability, this ability to absorb without losing the essential character of expression which is the soul of the African method. Soul determines the character of the human project and establishes the possibility of an integrated approach to research. It qualifies as a principle of procedure, a protocol of action in that it makes it possible for a scholar to examine any phenomenon from many angles. This eclecticism is welded into an integrated approach by soul.

The ancients understood that we were literally children of the earth, products of the organic system that is responsible for all we see. Humans were not of a different order from other materials of the earth. Since this was so it was clear to them that we were connected to everyone and everything. The fundamental mutability of cultures and civilizations never interferes with or contradicts the principle of human interconnectedness.

That soul represents a specific intervention in the methodological process is a point which must be conceded on the basis of the historical and cultural evidence of African American scholarly inquiry. Of course, it is arguable that this event is not so much an intervention as the natural state of human method prior to categorizing. In other words, the ancients who decided to gather berries from certain bushes and to reject others were, in effect, participating in the same process by which we discover answers and solutions. Thus, the soul of method is structure but not structure in the sense of which the structuralists speak.

Structuralism, even as a mode of thought, has taken on meaning in reference to the arrangement of parts such as in personality, architecture, and sentence structures. But the illusive structuralist mode can be traced to Piaget's attempt to identify three structural properties—wholeness, transformation, and self-regulation.[90] In his explanation Piaget claims that a structure is a system of transformations which involve laws which preserve and enrich the structure itself.[91]

The soul of method reveals itself in the formation of rhythm which is what I mean by a structure that is not the structure of the structuralists. Welsh-Asante expounds on the concept of rhythm as basic to the African aesthetic.[92] Her conceptualization of this phenomenon relates directly to the idea of the soul of method because what Piaget misses in his structuralist formulation is the idea of rhythms. The concepts of wholeness, transformation, and self-regulation are without movement although structuralism is considered the antithesis to formations built of aggregate elements. In this sense there is a false discourse bearing marks of betrayal of intellectual anticipation because to think of the constituents— wholeness, transformation, self-regulation—without rhythm is to see them as the very aggregation of elements that is anathema to the philosophical position of structuralism itself. Part of the arguments raised against such a fixed, structured approach to reality arises through the concern the Afrocentrist has with the "force vital" within process. The concern is toward the direction of the truly organic, fluid, agreeable nature of rhythm, the soul of method.

This becomes important when the scholar wishes to analyze the intricacies of the African American literary movements, or the nature of African American political power in urban centers, or the color issue among blacks in Brazil, or the European slave trade's disruption of the Guinea coast, or similar issues. Rhythm makes method responsive to a reality which is particularly efficacious if the scholar is able to tease out the insights which usually escape the mono-methodological perspective and Eurocentric approaches. One breaks the structured, lineal, monotony by investing research with soul, the rhythm of assessing and synthesizing in order to create understanding and meaning.

The acquisition of knowledge occurs within a social and political context defined by economic and historical factors. Thus, the individual scholar is engaged with the intersection of knowledge and the context. Not since Freud could a European scholar disclaim such an engagement. Indeed, Freud wrote that the scholar must examine himself and *his own position in history*, the motives—perhaps hidden motives—which have guided his choice of theme or period and his selection and interpretation of the facts, the *national and social background which has determined his angle of vision* .... [emphasis added][93]

Ultimately what this means is that history is relative, that ethnography is biography, that definitions are personal because the scholar is engaged with the acquisition of knowledge in a social way. I agree, however, with Preiswerk and Perrot that:

> To state that history is relative, both to the personality of the historian and to the society from which he sprang, does not mean one adopts a stance, in the epistemology of history in favor of historicism and against other schools. It is first of all an epistemological position external to history, according to which *all* knowledge is the product of the action of a subject (in relation to a "reality") and therefore is dependent on the cognitive behavior of this latter within a given social context.[94]

This raises the question of objectivity in research. Richards has pointed to the problems inherent in the concept which suggests that the scholar maintains a mental distance from the object of study. She shows that this is difficult to maintain and is at best an illusion. Why would a scholar want such a mental distance in the first place? Perhaps a more appropriate concept is decentration which is a process to reduce mental distance between subject and object of study. Although the Afrocentric method considers the separation of subject and object to be a transitory separation, the idea of a practical separation to allow engagement between scholar and subject is acceptable. In no case should a researcher deliberately falsify data for personal preferences. What becomes clear, however, in a study of numerous texts in the social sciences is that the Eurocentric writers have often written the prejudices of their societies into their texts. Many scholars have behaved toward African culture and history as pirates aboard a ship, they have taken as much as they could put under their belts and discarded the rest. The retrieval of African history remains the proper task of the Afrocentric scholars.

Delaney and Blyden: Pioneers of Proof

During the mid-nineteenth century, two scholar-scientists appeared who would establish the intellectual bases of the Afrocentric reclamation of African history, both on the continent and in the diaspora: Martin R. Delaney and Edward Wilmot Blyden. Both of these men were considered to be the very best the African people had produced in the Americas.

Martin Robinson Delaney, 1812-1885, was born in Charlestown, Virginia. There was perhaps no more contemporaneous African than Delaney. Pride of birth and race made him a veritable exception in his day. He knew that his heritage was Angola and Mandingo and that his grandfather had been a prince when he was captured by the slavers. Frederick Douglass speaking on Delaney's pride once remarked that "I thank God for making me a man simply; but Delaney always thanks him for making him a black man."[95]

Delaney's attitude was that there was no hope for the African unless each African felt palpitating in his or her heart the entire legacy of an historic people who abhorred slavery, prejudice, and every archaic and neanderthal idea about African inferiority.

Delaney believed that in the subjugation of the African the whites used two elements of historical deceit; one based on the constant rumor that whites were naturally superior to blacks; the other based on the corollary that blacks could not achieve in the intellectual realm. He presented himself as a formidable challenge to both arguments. In his person the deception was revealed and as a scientist, ethnologist, explorer, and medical doctor, Delaney demonstrated the most exacting obligation to the idea of African-centeredness.

Edward Wilmot Blyden, 1832-1912, attempted in a major way to address the fundamental issues of Africans in contact with Europeans and Arabs. In effect, Blyden wanted to demonstrate that the African, despite European propaganda, was not inferior to Europeans but was the progenitor of human civilization. Blyden published *Christianity, Islam and the Negro Race* in 1887, in which he defended the African's character, role in history, and potential for the future.[96]

Blyden saw Liberia, founded in 1822 by repatriated Africans from the United States, as a possible beachhead for the total recovery of the African spirit of industry. Having migrated from St. Thomas, Virgin Islands, where he was born, to Venezuela and then by the time he was eighteen to Liberia where he became a teacher and preacher, Blyden threw himself into the study of all aspects of African civilization and culture. He studied and taught Arabic, visiting the interior of Liberia where he found extensive libraries and learned men.

Several African studies concepts that have occurred in recent years found their early discussion by Blyden. Lynch has argued:

> Blyden portrayed the "African personality" as being the antithesis of that of the European, and serving to counter- act the worst aspects of the latter. The European character, according to Blyden, was harsh, individualistic, competitive and combative; European society was highly materialistic; the worship of science and technology was replacing that of God. In the character of the African, averred Blyden was to be found "the softer aspects of human nature"; cheerfulness, sympathy, willingness to serve, were some of its marked attributes. The special contribution of the African to civilization could be a spiritual one.[97]

The ideas of African personality, African spirituality and African salvation of the world are prevalent in Blyden's thought. He does not come to his conclusions on faith alone but rather argues that African geniuses are numerous and remarkable. Blyden lists Alexan- der Pushkin, Alexander Dumas, Touissant L'Ouverture, John Russwurm, Stephen Bashiel Warner, James Payne, Reverend J. W. C. Pennington, Reverend Samuel R. Ward, Frederick Doug- lass, Reverend Alexander Crummell as examples of the type of people produced by the African race.

> In view of such examples of intellectual and moral great- ness, as we have mentioned, shall such ordinary white men

as the majority of American slave-holders are, despite and insult the race from which they spring, and allege its inferiority, in justification of their most horrible system.[98]

Blyden's philosophical outlook was optimistic and he saw himself as part of a vanguard in the African world seeking to reconnect African peoples to their origins and history.

A notion latent in Blyden's interpretation of history which later became a dominant motif in Diop is the necessity for the African to reconstruct his or her world, a world cruelly distorted by Europe. In Diop the spirit was more revolutionary as it captured the rhythmic movement of Africa's call for liberation. On the heels of Fanon's war drums for violent overthrow of the oppressors and the neocolonialists, Diop emphatically announced that the time had come for the African to center his/her historical experiences and to stop operating on the periphery of Europe. The power of Diop's insistence gathered to him numerous critics, chief of whom were continental Africans trained in European academies, particularly Mazrui and Okpewho. Mazrui, like Diop, was a Muslim. He saw in Diop a rival for African Islamic intellectual hegemony. But Mazrui was no match for Diop in the breadth of his knowledge and the loyalty to African traditions as essential for African advancement.

The Cynic's Turn

Mazrui emerges at his height as a rhetorician capable of handling language in an eloquent fashion but his rhetoric is misleading due to internal ambiguity and an isolation from the discourse on method established by Afrocentrists. Indeed, his denial of this discourse has contributed to his ambiguity and the internal ambiguity results from his isolation. This is not to say that his political insights have been useless because they have been quite stimulating in their wit. My concern with Mazrui is more profound than a discussion of his rhetoric although it is impossible to avoid it.

Mazrui's cynicism about Africa colors his entire corpus; he is at once alienated and conflicted in his assessment of the political and historical phenomena he finds on the continent. This is not to say that he has not been perceptive but rather to point out that he has rarely advanced the idea of Africa. In effect, Mazrui becomes a truly Eurocentric Africanist of the genre that has been schooled in the discipline most advantageous to the advancement of a European intellectual particularism. What is valuable to note here is that African birth does not make one Afrocentric; Afrocentricity is a matter of intellectual discipline and must be learned and practiced. In Mazrui's case we see insight but not Afrocentric insight and one can certainly appreciate the quality of his wit and the manner of his style without acceding to him an Afrocentric perspective. Indeed, he is essentially an apologist for Arab penetration of Africa in cultural and political terms. Thus, the notion of the triple heritage of Africa as advanced in *The Africans* and other of his works. This formula is, however, an oversimplification since both the European and Arab or Christian and Muslim heritages are for the most part of recent origin. Certainly the Coptic traditions of Egypt and the Ge'ez traditions of Ethiopia are Christian without European influences dating from the first century; the Islamic heritage dates from the Arab invasion of Egypt in the seventh century A.D. However, the history of Africa reaches many thousands of years back from the period of the Christian and Islamic influences. What one could say with some degree of accuracy is that Christianity and Islam have been grafted upon the African heritage. One does not speak of the triple heritage of Europe, for example, even though millions of Muslims live in Europe as well as millions of Christians. In fact, if we took the major religions that are practiced in a region of the world and assessed the heritage of the region on the basis of those religions we would find that most areas of the world have a multiplicity of "influences." Mazrui is incorrect, however, in granting to Christianity and Islam the same place as the traditional and centering African culture found throughout the continent, perhaps less so in some places because of the density and intensity of the oppression and suppression of the indigenous people.

In effect, he does not transcend his particular vision of Africa because of an ideological entrapment: combining both European and Arab hegemonic positions over the intellectual and cultural resources of Africa. Indeed, Mazrui sees in Africa's enforced accommodation to Christianity and Islam a reason to rejoice that Africa demonstrates the possibility of "ecumenicalism."[99] Were he able to see Africa from an Afrocentric perspective he would question the imposition of Arabic or European influences on Africa, especially where those influences have disrupted the cultural, artistic, economic, and political lives of African peoples.

In his brilliant dissection of Mazrui's views, "The Fallacy of the 'Triple Heritage' Thesis: A Critique," Habtu argues that Mazrui's line of inquiry was Eurocentric. A more successful path to knowledge, he contends, might be to examine the African contribution and influence on Judaism, Arab, Western, Graeco-Roman and other civilizations.[100] Habtu says that "Diop, who incidentally is Muslim in background like Mazrui, was perhaps the first to suggest this approach in unequivocal terms in his book *The African Origin of Civilization*."[101] Habtu's critique is devastating for the Eurocentric Africanists led by Mazrui. He asserts that they speak of a Graeco-Roman or Judaeo-Christian heritage but do not choose to speak of Egypto-Hellenic, Egypto-Judaic, Nilo-Zairean or Nilo-Zairean-Sudanic heritage.[102] Of course, Mazrui is unable to think Afrocentrically and Habtu's criticism exposes Mazrui's inability to transcend the Africanist cocoon that views Africa as a receptor, a passive continent, incapable of influencing others and perhaps forever a beggar continent in term of ideas and concepts. There are reasons for Mazrui's difficulty with an Afrocentric perspective.

Mazrui's epigrammatic style, while often engaging, conceals the essentially liberal European orientation of his work. His critique of Africa is severed from any identifiable African school of thought. In fact, Mazrui assumes that he stands within no tradition in Africa but, of course, he is most traditional in his acceptance and practice of Eurocentric analysis of Africa. While this is properly not an African School of Thought it is framed in Africa and among Africans due to the heavy presence of European intellectual traditions on Africans.

Mazrui's ambiguity is directly related to his worldview. By conceiving of Africa as the receptor of others' views and ideologies he strips Africa of its productive and generative subjectivity. He sees the continent always as the acted-upon, victim, and powerless. His is an analysis of weakness where it is necessary to question the basis of strength. Mazrui's confusion is a liberal confusion found whenever the Afrocentrists call for the humanization of the world. Afrocentrists aim to see Africa as a part of the human equation in everything, to reject all attempts to take science, art, literature, music and theology out of Africa. Therefore, the work to humanize Africa, that is, to assist nature in transforming the environment for human fulfillment, is in the end not a plan to Africanize the world but to humanize it.

Despite Mazrui's own criticisms, Diop's conception of African-centeredness remains fundamental to the Afrocentric revolution because it redirected philosophical and historical inquiry to the role and place of Africa prior to Arab and European colonialism. Mazrui, for example, wants to start with Arab infiltration and to claim it as an equal legacy with the indigenous African contribution. Diop rejects this view as unscientific.

We must begin from the perspective that sees post-Diopan Afrocentricity as the intellectual movement which restored the place of Africans in world history and reestablished the human project in terms consonant to a critique of knowledge from African-centeredness. And yet we cannot speak of post-Diopan in a strict sense because this is the age of Diop without whom the dignity of Africans would have continued to be defended, as DuBois admirably did, by appeals to Eurocentric frames of reference. Diop freed us from that dependence. He argued that the objectivity of knowledge referred to by European scholars could not be separated from consciousness of the social-cultural world and that Europeans brought that consciousness with them whenever they discussed Africa. This is why Hegel's knowledge of Africa is dimmed by his participation in the European conception of Africa; this is why the African, freed from the social-cultural consciousness imposed by European education can see the brightness of his/her own history.

African American scholars have been the principal proponents of Diop's ideas, although on the continent Theophile Obenga, Director of the CICIBA, and the European, Martin Bernal, have advanced various aspects of Diop's historiography. Chief among the African American scholars are the Pan-Africanists: Yosef Ben-Jochannan, Hunter Adams, John Henrik Clarke, Asa Hilliard,

Charles Finch, Maulana Karenga, Wade Noble, and Jacob Carruthers.[103]

The Cultural Issue

I have said that acquisition of knowledge occurs in a cultural context. What, then, is culture? In the sense that the Afrocentrists speak of it culture refers to the learned and shared values, attitudes, predispositions, and behavior patterns of a human group which can be transmitted. Thus, I consider world voices, world views, cosmogonies, institutions, ideas, myths, epics, and symbols as comprising culture.

The preservation of knowledge depends upon retentive mechanisms such as human memory, computers, writing systems, video and audio recorders on one level and libraries, repositories, museums, and archives another level. Writing, however, has become a major avenue for retention and preservation. Ngugi has explained how writing ought to be viewed:

> Writing is representation of sounds with visual symbols, from the simplest knot among shepherds to tell the number in a herd or the hieroglyphics among the Agikuyu gicaandi singers and poets of Kenya, to the most complicated and different letter and picture writing systems of the world today.[104]

The valorization of European letters and the degradation of African letters, writing, communication systems and visions show, as in the case of Kamuzu Banda's setting up of a Malawian private school where Africans cannot teach, the most servile intellectual behavior on the part of Africans. Banda embodies by virtue of this example of self-hatred, the most violent form of anti-African ideas. He established the Kamuzu Academy to train young Malawians in English. But no Malawian was allowed to teach at Kamuzu when it opened in 1982.

> It is a grammar school designed to produce boys and girls who will be sent to universities like Harvard, Chicago,

Oxford, Cambridge and Edinburgh and be able to compete on equal terms with others elsewhere.

The President has instructed that Latin should occupy a central place in the curriculum. All teachers must have had at least some Latin in their academic background. Dr. Banda has often said that no one can fully master English without knowledge of languages such as Latin and French. . . . [105]

From the European center, Africa was seen as marginal, uncivilized and on the periphery of historical consciousness. Some of the statements of European writers reveal the extent of their attack on African intelligence. Examine the works of

such geniuses of racism as a Rider Haggard or a Nicholas Monsarrat; not to mention the pronouncement of some of the giants of Western intellectual and political establishment, such as Hume (". . . the negro is naturally inferior to the whites . . . "), Thomas Jefferson (". . . the blacks . . . are inferior to the whites endowments of both body and mind . . . "), or Hegel with his Africa comparable to a land of childhood still enveloped in the dark mantle of the night as far as the development of self-conscious history was concerned. [106]

Foundations of an Approach

The practical reasons for advancing an Afrocentric method are found in the manner Africa has been studied by Africanists. Since the Eurocentric methods have been aggressive and violative, it is necessary to demonstrate a humanistic method capable of allowing for the acquisition of data from all societies, American, European, Asian and African.

Almost definitionally, the method will have to deal with the question of exploitation of data, transformation of data, theft of data, and distortion of data. Ngugi wa Thiong'o has maintained that the "cultural bomb" is more damaging to a people than the military and economic weapons. [107]

He eloquently describes the impact of this intellectual and cultural war on Africa in these words:

> The effect of a cultural bomb is to annihilate a people's belief in their names, in their languages, in their environment, in their heritage of struggle, in their unity, in their capacities and ultimately in themselves. It makes them see their past as one wasteland of nonachievement and it makes them want to distance themselves from that wasteland. It makes them want to identify with that which is furthest removed from themselves; for instance, with other peoples' languages rather than their own. It makes them identify with that which is decadent and reactionary, all those forces which would stop their own springs of life. It even plants serious doubts about the moral rightness of struggle. Possibilities of triumph or victory are seen as remote, ridiculous dreams. The intended results are despair, despondency and a collective death-wish. Amidst this wasteland which it has created, imperialism presents itself as the cure and demands that the dependant sing hymns of praise with the constant refrain: "Theft is holy." Indeed, this refrain sums up the new creed of the neo-colonial bourgeoisie in many "independent" African states.[108]

Ngugi's "cultural bomb" was dropped on Africa long ago. Its ramifications have fallen-out over the entire scope of knowledge about the continent, poisoning the streams of inquiry as well as the fountains of truth. Chinweizu in *Decolonising the African Mind* concludes that Africans have seldom stood their ground to defend their customs, culture, or economies. According to Chinweizu both Europeans and Arabs have exploited the continent because Africans have not been able to establish a collective sense of responsibility. Chinweizu believes that the cultural bombardments by Europe and Arabia have taken their toll on African will to overcome.[109]

Herodotus and Africa

Some European historians have quarrelled with the writings of Herodotus and others in an attempt to undermine Africa's contri-

butions to world civilization. Other scholars have introduced
spurious concepts, that is, they have invented illusive concepts and
tried to invest them with meaning to create confusion around
African phenomena. Africalogists study all branches of knowledge
with the aim of throwing Afrocentric light on African phenomena.
Therefore, it is proper to consider the works of Herodotus as
pertinent to our understanding.

Herodotus was the most comprehensive of the early European
recorders of the customs, traditions, and civilizations of North
Africa. In the fifth century B.C., Herodotus observed four distinct
groups of people in the part of Africa where he travelled. Two
groups were indigenous to Africa; the other two groups were
foreign to the continent. The indigenous people Herodotus called
Ethiopians and Libyans. The foreign people were Phoenicians and
Greeks. The latter had been influenced by the customs of the
Africans. Both the Libyans and Ethiopians (Herodotus considered
the Egyptians to be a branch of the Ethiopian people) spoke a
similar Hamitic language. As John Jackson says, "Anyone who
speaks a Hamitic language is a Hamite, and there is no necessary
racial connotation involved. But certainly the idea widely entertained, that the ancient Hamites of Africa were of caucasoid origin
in demonstrably untenable."[110] Indeed Harry Johnston, who is cited
widely on the Hamites defined them as:

> That Negroid race which was the main stock of the ancient
> Egyptian, and is represented at the present day by the
> Somali, the Galla and some of the blood of Abyssinia and
> of Nubia, and perhaps by the peoples of the Sahara
> Desert.[111]

As Bernal has shown in *Black Athena* that Herodotus considered Africa as the land of the blacks. Indeed, Herodotus' account
of an expedition of young African men from the Nasamonian
region who travelled across the Sahara to the Niger River is most
explicit:

> They said there had grown up among them some wild
> young men, the sons of certain chiefs, when they came to

man's estate, indulged in all manner of extravagances, and among other things drew lots for five of their number to go and explore the desert parts of Libya, and try if they could not penetrate further than any had done previously. The young men therefore, despatched, on this errand by their comrades with a plentiful supply of water and provisions, travelled at first through the inhabited region, passing which they came to the wild beast tract, whence they finally entered upon the desert, which they proceeded to cross in a direction from east to west. After journeying for many days over a wide extent of sand, they came at last to a plain where they observed trees growing; approaching them, and seeing fruit on them, they proceeded to gather it. While they were thus engaged, there came upon them some dwarfish men, under the middle height, who seized them and carried them off. The Nasamonians could not understand a word of the language, nor had they any acquaintance with the language of the Nasamonians. They were led across extensive marshes and finally came to a town, where all the men were of the height of their conductors, and black complexioned. A great river flowed by the town, running from west to east and containing crocodiles.[112]

The Rise of the Oriental Question

The destruction of Carthage in 146 B.C. by the Romans meant a permanent settlement of Romans on the northern coast of Africa for several hundred years. The Romans referred to the indigenous Libyans and Ethiopians as *barbari* (barbarians) from which the modern term Berber is derived. In actuality the Berber are a mixture of the indigenous Africans with Romans, Phoenicians, and Greeks. The name did not imply inferiority to the Romans but those whose traditions and customs were different. The people of North Africa, like most other Africans, had a matrilineal type of social order which was in contradistinction to the Roman system.

Roman conquest of Carthage was assisted by the Numidians and Mauritanians who wanted to end Carthaginian hegemony over their territories. J. C. DeGraft-Johnson writes that

The Numidian and Mauritanian kings and chiefs allied themselves to the Romans because they desired home rule of self-government, and for that reason they wanted the power of Carthage destroyed, as Carthaginian influence was already making itself felt in their internal and external affairs. But no sooner had the Numidian kings and chiefs assisted Rome to destroy Carthage than Rome picked a quarrel with them and annexed their country. The Mauritanian kings, who occupied part of modern Morocco and Algeria, had hoped to exercise self-determination and enjoy full self-government, but this was not to be. Within the hundred-odd years from the fall of Carthage in 146 B.C. to 42 B.C., Rome incorporated or absorbed into her Empire the regions equivalent to western Tripolitania, Tunisia, and all the coastal regions of Algeria and Morocco. Rome also annexed the old Greek colonies in Cyrenaica, and in 30 B.C. added the newly acquired territory of Egypt to the Cyrenaican possessions in order to form a Roman province.[113]

DeGraft-Johnson's discussion of the events of Morocco, Mauritania and Algeria throw into relief additional intellectual problems of knowledge. DeGraft-Johnson sees the ancient northern African lands as African yet the entire northern African question, since the Aryan model was initiated takes on what is referred to as an East-West axis.

One of the abiding intellectual problems in the West is the artificial division of philosophical reality into Eastern and Western spheres. Typically a discussion of this sort begins with "a basic distinction between east and west as the starting point for elaborate theories, epics, novels, social descriptions, and political accounts concerning the Orient, its people, customs, 'mind,' destiny, and so on."[114] Although Edward Said has written a provocative account of the discourse on Orientalism he is as much a victim of the artificial division of philosophical reality as the Westerners he so ably criticizes. The principal problem with Said is that he has bought into the invisibility of Africa and has claimed classical Africa as a part of the Orient, largely by relying on writers who expressed a hostility to Africa and Africans during the seventeenth, eighteenth, and nineteenth centuries. Moreover, in trying to prove that "European culture gained in strength and identity by setting itself off against the Orient,"[115] he followed in Europe's footsteps by misunderstanding Africa and misplacing a part of Africa in the Orient. In fact, Said writes that:

> There is very little consent to be found, for example, in the fact that Flaubert's encounter with an Egyptian courtesan produced a widely influential model of the Oriental woman; she never spoke of herself, she never represented her emotions, presence, or history. *He* spoke for and represented her. He was foreign, comparatively wealthy, male, and these were historical facts of domination that allowed him not only to possess Kuchuk Hanem physically but to speak for her and tell his readers in what way she was "typically Oriental." My argument is that Flaubert's situation of strength in relation to Kuchuk Hanem was not an isolated instance. It fairly stands for the pattern of relative strength between East and West, and the discourse about the Orient that it enabled.[116]

But when he writes thusly he is speaking about Arabs in Egypt, an African country. In other words, Said claims Egypt for the Orient in much the same way the French had done in the eighteenth century after Napoleon's invasion. To further tie Africa to the Orient, Said uses Egypt in conjunction with India, which could properly be referred to as a part of the Orient. In fact, Said writes:

> I doubt that it is controversial, for example, to say that an Englishman in India or Egypt in the later nineteenth century took an interest in those countries that was never far from their status in his mind as British colonies. To say this may seem quite different from saying that all academic knowledge about India and Egypt is somehow tinged and impressed with, violated by, the gross political fact—and yet *that is what I am saying* in this study of Orientalism. [emphasis in original][117]

What is perhaps most peculiar is Said's submission to the attempt to connect Sanskrit and the Indo-Aryan language project in such a way as to take Egypt out of Africa. In other words, the classical African civilizations of the Nile Valley came to be seen in a conceptual way, in Said's thinking, as attached to India and Sanskrit studies, further divorcing Egypt from Africa. Said says

> Yet at certain moments of that general European history of interest in the East, particular parts of the Orient like Egypt, Syria, and Arabia cannot be discussed without also studying Europe's involvement in the more distant parts, of which Persia and India are the most important; a notable case in point is the connection between Egypt and India so far as eighteenth- and nineteenth-century Britain was concerned. Similarly, the French role in deciphering the Zend-Avesta, the preeminence of Paris as a center of Sanskrit studies during the first decade of the nineteenth century, the fact that Napoleon's interest in the Orient was contingent upon his sense of the British role in India: all these Far Eastern interests directly influenced French interest in the Near East, Islam, and the Arabs.[118]

For all his clarity in exposing the European prosecution of a false discourse on Orientalism, Said is terribly confused on the issue of Egypt. Distinction must be made between ancient Egypt and Arabic Egypt. The latter being a rather recent, in terms of African history, political and cultural hegemony on the indigenous population. However, the preceding passage demonstrates an attempt to totally dismiss the presence of Africans. In order to write such a passage Said has to buy into the very same discourse he endeavors to overthrow. But since his aim is to vindicate the Arabs against the Europeans he leaves Africans invisible in the process. This does not work except as a further obfuscation of the Kemetic reality. Said could have profited from reading the works of Diop whom he obviously does not know. Nevertheless, he mentions the inclination of H. A. R. Gibbs, an eminent student of Arabic, to call himself an Orientalist instead of an Arabist when in fact he was most particularly an Arabist.[119] But Said is particularly incorrect regarding the place of Sanskrit when he adds to the mythology of the preeminence of Sanskrit as a language. The question is preeminent to what? Research has long since demonstrated the anteriority of ancient Mdu Neters to African languages and its primacy as a civilizing language. Despite this Said is content to write

> When around the turn of the eighteenth century the Orient definitively revealed the age of its languages—thus outdating Hebrew's divine pedigree—it was a group of Europeans who made the discovery, passed it on to other scholars, and preserved the discovery in the new science of Indo-European philology.[120]

A proper critique would have demonstrated that the Indo-European philological school did not possess the antiquity of the ancient African pharaonic language and that the so-called Orient language was African. Said does comment that:

> As early as 1804 Benjamin Constant noted in his _Journal intime_ that he was not about to discuss India in his _De la religion_ because the English who owned the place and the Germans who studied it indefatigably had made India the _fons et origo_ of everything; and then there were the French who had decided after Napoleon and Champollion that everything originated in Egypt.[121]

The truth of the matter is that Egypt predates Indian civilization and language by several thousands of years.

Although some consider the commencement of Orientalism to be found in the decision of the Church Council of Vienna in 1312 to establish chairs in Arabic, Greek, Hebrew, and Syriac at Paris, Oxford, Bologna, Avignon and Salamanca[122] the real period of the movement to take Egypt out of Africa and place it in the Orient was the nineteenth century when Princeton, Chicago, Pennsylvania, London, Paris and Berlin founded schools of Oriental studies.

Quite frankly, the only reason Egypt is considered by Said as a part of the Orient is the Arabic language, a language not indigenous to Africa. Arabic, Turkish, and Persian (Farsi) were studied by d'Herbelot, Galland, and Hottinger, either separately or as a group, in what was to be called oriental studies. Although Arabic was spoken in Egypt, it was not the original or ancient Egyptian language.

It should be noted, however, that Napoleon developed an Institut d'Égypte soon after the 1799 invasion. This institute was soon to be overshadowed by the various schools of Oriental studies. As European knowledge of Africa increased, its hostility toward the classical civilizations of the Nile became more complex.

Nowhere has the pantheon of distinguished icons of cultural faith been more rewarding for seekers than ancient Africa. In classical Africa one finds the world of the Sphinx, Isis, Osiris, Horus, Kagemni, Keti, Nefertari, Hatshepsut, Rameses, Prester John, Imhotep, Tutankhamen, Seti, Piankhy, and Tarharka. No region on earth was any richer for the seeker after ancient truths.

Napoleon's aim in Africa was to subdue Egypt and thereby gain access to the glory of classical Africa. A byproduct was to be the outmaneuvering of Britain. The Treaty of Campo Formio behind him in 1797, while in Italy Napoleon plotted for the overthrow of Egypt. Fascinated in his youth by Egypt and particularly the conquest by Alexander of the country in the fourth century B.C., Napoleon saw himself as the new Alexander reconquering the most ancient part of Africa. The fact that Egypt's culture had become essentially a new Islamic outpost further intrigued him since he could begin to repay the Muslims for their long occupation of Spain, Sicily and portions of France. He relied upon French scholars to assess the difficulty of taking Egypt.

Napoleon's enlistment of several dozen "savants" for his Egyptian Expedition is too well known to require detail here. His idea was to build a sort of living archive for the expedition, in the form of studies conducted on all topics by the members of the Institut d'Égypte, which he founded. What is perhaps less well known is Napoleon's prior reliance upon the work of the Comte de Volney, a French traveler whose *Voyage en Égypte et en Syrie* appeared in two volumes in 1787.[123]

Napoleon refers to Volney in his own memoirs *Campagnes d'Égypte et de Syrie, 1798-1799* which were dictated while he was held at Saint Helena. He used every device to gain the advantage for the Armée d'Égypte, even to the extent of telling the Muslims of Egypt that the French army were the true Muslims. Convinced that a demonstration of piety would win over the Muslims, Napoleon made a proclamation in Alexandria on July 2, 1798, in order to show that he was in support of Islam! Later just to emphasize his belief in Islam, Napoleon tried to underscore his scheme by convincing the Muslim teachers of his sincerity.

> To this end, the sixty ulemas who taught at the Azhar were invited to his quarters, given full military honors, and then allowed to be flattered by Napoleon's admiration for Islam and Mohammed and by his obvious veneration for the Koran, with which he seemed perfectly familiar. This worked, and soon the population of Cairo seemed to have lost its distrust of the occupiers.[124]

The most daring part of Napoleon's occupation was the thoroughness with which he intended to conquer the culture of Egypt. No conqueror prior to him had been so ruthless in his scheme to gain dominance over the legacy of the ancients. Indeed, after the Roman Empire, the Byzantine Empire, the Arabs, and the Mamelukes had all occupied Egypt for a while. Although the Arabs had been in Egypt the longest and their influence on the culture was most telling their occupation never possessed the aggressive character of Napoleon's adventure. While the Arabs neglected African history by occupying the land with little interest in the history, the Armée d'Égypte occupied the history of Egypt and sought to record, study, dissect, and appropriate the whole of the civilization. In the massive work, *Description de l'Égypte*, published between 1809 and 1828 in twenty three volumes, the French attempted to demonstrate their total acquisition of Egypt intellectually.

Egypt captured the French imagination and made Jean-Baptiste-Joseph Fourier, an author of the *Preface Historique* to the *Descrip-*

tion de l'Égypte, exclaim on the significance of Egypt to knowledge
in Europe.

> Placed between Africa and Asia, and communicating
> easily with Europe, Egypt occupies the center of the an-
> cient continent. This country presents only great memories;
> it is the homeland of the arts and conserves innumerable
> monuments; its principal temples and the palaces inhabited
> by its kings still exist, even though its least ancient edifices
> had already been built by the time of the Trojan War,,
> Homes, Lycurgus, Solon, Pythagoras, and Plato all went to
> Egypt to study the sciences, religion, and the laws. Alexan-
> der founded an opulent city there, which for a long time
> enjoyed commercial supremacy and which witnessed
> Pompey, Caesar, Mark Antony, and Augustus deciding
> between them the fate of Rome and that of the entire
> world. It is therefore proper for this country to attract the
> attention of illustrious princes who rule the destiny of
> nations.
>
> No considerable power was ever amassed by any
> nation, whether in the West or in Asia, that did not also
> turn that nation toward Egypt, which was regarded in
> some measure as its natural lot.[125]

The act of grabbing Egypt for Europe or for the "Orient" was
a frontal attack on Africa. The fact that the early Greeks studied in
Egypt meant that the annexation of Egypt to Europe was seen as
natural. The imagination of Europe was riveted by the French being
in Egypt. Fourier could write that when the news of the French in
Egypt came to the Europeans they were astounded, the great
project had been meditated in silence and only when it was successful had it been announced to the world.

It is important for an understanding of the confusion surrounding the methods of "Africanists" to note that they have seldom
challenged the "orientalist" myth. Despite sharp divergences among
some of them they have nevertheless advanced an interpretation of
Africa that favors the orientalist explanation. This they have often
done in spite of efforts to assert a positive view of Africa. Unfortu-

nately two continental African "Africanists" have made some of the most incredible assertions.

Sulayman Nyang's *Islam, Christianity, and African Identity* attempts to examine the interaction of Islam and Christianity in Africa. Nyang's analysis leaps toward an Afrocentric account of that interaction. However, he is trapped by his own identification with Islam and consequently misconstrues the nature of the Abrahamic tradition's intrusion into Africa. In his method Nyang is similar to Mazrui, both insist on the three heritages of Africa, meaning traditional, Islamic and Christian. Both fail to grasp the impact of intrusions on African culture. Nyang believes that in some respects this invasion may be valuable to Africa.

> In my view, the African encounter with the Abrahamic tradition has been very inspiring and spiritually elevating. The message of Abraham, as echoed and preached by the Old Testament prophets, Christ and Muhammad, is still reverberating in the African spiritual firmaments. The ringing of church bells and the booming voices of latter-day Bilals summoning fellow believers to prayer, make it crystal clear to all observers that Africa has finally joined the growing commonwealth of believers in the Abrahamic tradition. The African decision to embrace the Abrahamic tradition is significant in many respects ....
>
> To put it another way, I would say that the African encounter with the Abrahamic tradition is going to be, in the long run, beneficial to the Africans as well as their fellow worshippers elsewhere on the planet. Africa's gift to the followers of the Abrahamic tradition will be the spirit of cultural tolerance in a world of ethnic diversity.[125]

There is no triple heritage of Africa, there is the double legacy of Islam and Christianity impacting on the indigenous culture of the continent emerging as "double trouble" for African expression. Nyang goes so far as to say, "In my view, the key concept in traditional African thought is the cosmic schizophrenic tendencies of man."[126] Nyang explains that this means the world of concrete reality, the world of social values, and the world of inexpressible spiritual powers. While there is a basis for Nyang's philosophical divisions in the ethical system of Africa there is no justification for calling these divisions "cosmic schizophrenic tendencies" as if they reflect a psychological disorder. Such discourse about traditional African society betrays Nyang's difficulty in resolving his own dilemma. For example, he calls African emphasis on social values and the traditions of the ancestors an "overemphasis."[128] Or take his conclusion that Arabic succeeded in becoming the language of the north of Africa because of "its prestige and usefulness."[129] While that is partly true, it is more correct to say that the language succeeded because of force and punishment.

Like Mazrui, Nyang's religion seems to get in the way of his thinking. He knows he is in trouble when he writes:

> In fact, in talking about the Islamic contribution to the social universe of the African, one could argue that the arrival of Islam in the continent widened the horizons of the traditional African a little bit. Whereas in the past this man had entrusted destiny to the hands of the spirits who resided in a well, a tree or a stream somewhere in the ecological setting of his tribal group, whereas he wished to placate the gods and ancestors, under the Islamic religion he found that his life was for appointed time and that his deeds on earth did have singular meaning.[130]

Nyang is, of course, carried away with the valorization of Islam. He writes:

> Another area where the early Muslims could have affected the minds and hearts of the traditional Africans was their possession of the powers of the written word. This technology of intellectual conservation must have deeply impressed their early African hosts in the West Sudan, for it must have looked like a miracle to them that a man could reduce long court proceedings into signs and symbols.[131]

Any Afrocentric method would begin with the consciousness of the African populations rather than the "imposed" consciousness of the Muslims. No assessment has been made of the values, beliefs, and attributes of the culture of Africans before Nyang tells us that the Africans must have thought the reduction of court proceedings to signs and symbols was miraculous. Obviously the writer neither understands nor appreciates the diversity and complexity of African graphic systems.

Furthermore, I cannot see why the Muslim missionaries should not have thought it "miraculous" that the African judges could sit for three days listening to arguments of adversaries and then present those arguments verbatim to the satisfaction of the principals. What Nyang has done here is to take the Eurocentric valorization of alphabetism as his leading concept. For Nyang, the African is the only one "reduced" to wonderment. The Afrocentric Africalogist, basing analysis on concrete human behaviors, discovers interactive wonderment on the parts of all parties. Without such a view, the scholar simply assumes ideas, concepts and terms imposed by European writers to be a priori correct. One sees the danger of this blind allegiance to "concepts" in the use of the word "negro," for example.

The Use of the Term "Negro"

There is no ethnic group in Africa that calls itself *negro* or its language *negro*. The term is preeminently a creation of the European mind to refer to any African group or people who correspond to a certain negative image of culture. The term is meaningless in reality but has become a useful word for those who would serve a political purpose by the term. Thus, the word "negro" is used by white writers to obfuscate as in the following examples: "Some such movements are probably reflected in the ever recurrent tradition that the early dynasties of Egypt were of Ethiopian origin. It is perhaps too often assumed that 'Ethiopian' is necessarily the equivalent of 'negro.'"[132] Here, for example, in a book published in 1967, MacMichael is debating with history. He uses the term "negro" as it is an inferior people. Ethiopians (Shoa, Amhara, Galla, etc.) are one branch of the African people as Egyptians and Zulu and Yoruba are branches of the African people. "Negro" on the other hand is introduced to obscure the Africanness of the classical Pharaonic civilizations.

The European writers often translated the ancient texts in the light of their contemporary political realities. No ancient African text mentions the word "negro." It simply does not exist, but the European writers took liberty to empower certain expressions in the texts with their own social conventions. Consider MacMichael's discussion of the origin of the ethnic name Nuba.

> This term first occurs in literature in the geography of Eratosthenes, who was born in 287 B.C. He speaks of "the Nuba." Later the name occurs as Nubato, or in the Latinized form of Nobatae.
>
> The ultimate derivation of the word is not known, but it appears to be of very ancient origin and may be connected through the Coptic NOYBT (Meaning "to plait") with "*nebved*," the word used in the inscription of Thothmes I (date c. 1540 B.C.) to denote "the plaited-haired ones," or as it is perhaps with less accuracy translated "the curly-haired ones" whom that monarch overthrew in the neighbourhood of the third cataract: "He hath overthrown the chief of the Nubians; the Negro [*nehesi*] is helpless.... There is not a remnant among the curly-haired, who came to attack him."[133]

The rendering of "nehesi" as "negro" is typical of the use of terms which had no meaning for Africans. Perhaps the best example of MacMichael's racist subtleties is revealed in the following statement:

> It may be the case, and probably is, that the southern NUBA are to some extent the modern representatives of the race of negroes who temporarily held Dongola and the cataract country south of Halfa in the days of the Middle Kingdom and early Empire and whose congeners, no doubt at a later date, formed part of the forces of the Ethiopian dynasty that conquered Egypt and ruled it for something less than a century, but these negroes were aliens in the

northern Sudan and most of them were forced back to the south, and their place in Lower Nubia was taken by its original inhabitants and settlers from Egypt.[134]

The writer has and gives no evidence for the preceding statement. It is purely based on the social realities of the writer. Again the use of "negroes" obfuscates the African reality. Furthermore, the "race of negroes" he speaks of are Africans, as are the Nuba of whom he is writing. The statement that "these negroes were aliens" is incredible inasmuch as the people of the Sudan were Africans and without giving an ethnic name one cannot say whether these people were aliens or not. There is no negro ethnic group or race. The intellectual confusion which reigns in the use of racial classifications by scholars who apply contemporary social conventions is seen in statements like the following:

> The Middle Nubian stock was also mixed, it is probable, with another strain, that of the red-skinned BEGA from the eastern deserts. But in the main, from Assuan for some distance south of Halfa, it was negroid, though certainly not true negro.[135]

Do these "negroes" have culture, language, civilization? Are they without a name other than the modern European creation negro?

MacMichael's is unrepentant, he reaches back to Kashta, the African who had his capital at Gebel Barkal (Napata) in 750 B.C. and claims, with no evidence given, that Kashta, one of the great leaders of Africa invaded Egypt and established his supremacy as far as Thebes and had under his control subjects who were Nubians of the present darker type and negroes or semi-negroes.[136] Of course, this is nonsense since Africans have always come in many complexions. Furthermore, these so-called negroes or semi-negroes appear in no concrete manner anywhere in Africa.

In another passage in a similar vein MacMichael says "I am strongly inclined to think that the Nobatae (Nubians) were once lords of the Bayuda and the country south of it and that their negro ancestors may have previously ousted the Libyan races therefrom, or, more probably, become fused with them in race."[137]

This is not enough. MacMichael is afraid that the Africans who ruled Egypt were "of the same stock as these negro ancestors" of the Nubians.[138] Perhaps the most creative use of obfuscation occurs in the following passage:

> One may say then that when the Muhammadan Arabs invaded Lower Nubia in the seventh century A.D. they found there a race radically compounded of predynastic Egyptian and cognate Hamitic elements blended with dynastic Egyptian and Libyan stocks and deeply and repeatedly modified by forty centuries of dilution with Negro blood.[139]

Four thousands years of "dilution with Negro blood" means that whomever the people were they possessed the characteristics of the so-called Negroes.

Even the early Basil Davidson could not avoid the use of the "negro" illusion. There was no other possibility, it seems, for him at the time. Thus he writes "These people, these 'negroes' (for neat racial pigeonholes have little application here), undoubtedly multiplied in the years after about 5000 B.C."[140] Fortunately, Davidson lived long enough to correct most of his early references to "negroes" for the African people in all of their varieties may be referred to by their ethnic or linguistic names, i.e., Yoruba, Sao, Fulbe, Balondo, Bamenda, etc., rather than by imposed designations such as Hamitic, Negro, Bantu, etc. These Eurocentric determinations alienate and distort the historical achievements of the African people. Numerous other writers have fallen into the same intellectual trap.

Churchward, for all of his great industry in tracking African origins, also falls in line with the "negro" theory contending that there is a "Masaba negro" and a "Nilotic negro," the latter, according to him, following the first in evolution but never becoming the first.[141] This, of course, is as nonsensical as saying the "Alpine" or "Nordic" preceded the other in evolution never becoming the other. These concepts have no real basis in science. Africans of a particular geo-cultural region can be spoken of but

not in terms of Eurocentric illusions. Unfortunately, Churchward
was fundamentally a racist.

Khaldunic Ethnocentrism in History

Viewed from the vast field of history Churchward can be seen
as a part of a larger stream of historians, beginning with Khaldun,
who misunderstood and misrepresented Africa and Africans. In *The
MuQaddimah: An Introduction to History*, Khaldun wrote that
Sudanese "are in general characterized by levity, excitability, and
great emotionalism. They are found eager to dance whenever they
hear a melody."[141] Furthermore, the Egyptians are said to be like
the Sudanese, Zanj, and Abyssinians for they "are dominated by
joyfulness, levity and disregard for the future."[142] Khaldun spends
considerable time citing stereotypes about the Abyssinians, Zanj,
and Sudanese only to report that all the stereotypes he had heard
remain "inconclusive and unproven."[143]

Khaldun's history does not consider the presence of African
civilization in Egypt (Kemet) at all. He begins his analysis with the
Greeks thus laying a foundation for Western historians to ignore
the Kemetic foundation of Greek civilization. We are, therefore, left
with Khaldun's incomplete and imprecise history as a basis for
much racist propaganda. In addition, Khaldun's ideas on historiography underscore the significance of writing in episodic history and
set the stage for the dichotomy between prehistory and history.
More contemporary scholars have seen Africa in a different light
both in terms of the richness of its archaeological record and the
abundance of its oral histories.

History/Prehistory

The Afrocentrist cannot utilize the Khaldunian notion of
history and prehistory where history only begins with writing and
there is a sense that prehistory contains nothing of significance to
human civilization. Too much of Western history is essentially the
history of the written record. We know, of course, that the African
record in what is called prehistory is extensive and fruitful for an
understanding of contemporary societies. In Africa there is unlimited evidence of early human development. There is also the fact that
methodological and disciplinary questions raised by archaeologists

might be answered by the African record. In newer works, scholars are beginning to appreciate the antiquity of the African record.

The archaeologists and prehistorians of other regions have much to learn from the African record, not only from its unparalleled evidence for the earliest periods of human development, but also methodologically. Because most of Africa has undergone environmental change on a scale which is relatively minor when compared with the glaciated regions of Eurasia and North America, abundant data are fairly easily available to aid the interpretation of prehistoric subsistence practices. Africa also provides excellent opportunities for contrasting the testimony of archaeology with that of linguistic and oral historical studies, and for interpreting the meaning of rock art in the light of the belief systems of recent peoples.[145]

I mean the definitions of history and prehistory cannot turn on the pejorative attribution to societies rich in other than written evidences. Much data exist in Africa to assist in organizing a cohesive record of human civilization. Indeed, Phillipson says prehistory may not even be appropriate a concept for Africa.

The period of time before written history is conventionally known as prehistory. The term is not entirely appropriate for Africa, for a number of reasons. First, there were long periods, especially in the northern part of the continent, about which written records, although available, are not generally informative on many aspects of contemporary life. There are also numerous instances where the only available written records were produced by outsiders and frequently given an incomplete account of matters which the writers did not properly understand. These are situations which confront prehistorians in many parts of the world, but they give rise to particular problems in some parts of Africa because of the generally shallow time-depth of indigenous literacy. A different approach is required to those aspects of African culture which, to a very large extent, take the place of written literature in other regions. These include the developed oral traditions which, in many societies, preserve the accumulated wisdom of the people, including details of their past history. Again, language itself plays a large part in determining a people's or an individual's sense of identity. Where written examples of ancient languages do not exist, much can be learned through the study of present-day linguistic forms and distributions concerning the nature and interactions of past populations.[146]

Beyond this, however, is a more pointed conceptual problem. The criterion of written transmission of knowledge as history is problematic because

> The acceptance of the criterion obliges, historians, perplexed by "preliterate" societies, to exclude a large number of non-Western cultures from history. The conceptual cleavage, prehistory-history, leads Western historians to assert the ahistoricity of these cultures *in the contemporary epoch*! (emphasis added)[147]

Preiswerk and Perrot recognize that history as taught in the West is essentially the history of the West with appendices to other peoples. They have, therefore, proposed a distinction between History and history.

> We believe that History means the classic narratives, particularly in textbooks, which come out strongly on the side of the West, and omit nearly everything that might enhance other cultures. In short, History is ethnocentric. We spell the word with a capital H in order to indicate that it is still predominant. It is this representation of the past, at least according to the analysis we made of the texts, which is taught to one generation after another in Western countries. It is History which appears to be perfectly integrated with the underlying ideologies of industrial society. In this respect it performs a legitimizing

function both of perpetuating this society and justifying the
type of relations established with other societies.[148]

Yet Africa remains central to any discussion of human society and
the methodologists seeking to establish an entry into any field of
human development in an historical manner must consult the
African evidence. That evidence may be found in many places.
Principally, however, it is the oral record that is most important in
order to properly interpret African traditions.[149] The function of the
oral historical tradition in African societies tend to be to support
the state, to give official explanations of events, and to preserve the
accepted versions of the group's history.

In addition to the oral traditions which contain official records
of various societies, the fossilized evidence of these societies has
really only begun to be explored. Areas of central Africa, Zaire,
Uganda, Malawi, and Angola remain to be fully studied in connection with human society. Recent research has established beyond a
doubt that between 6.0 and 4.0 million years ago the first so-called
homonids appeared in Africa. Phillipson contends that "virtually all
the important fossils which illustrate this development have been
recovered from sites in eastern and southern Africa."[150] *Austra-
lopithecus robustus* and *A. boisei* are regional African races because
the first is found in South Africa and the latter in East Africa.

Discussions of hominids and oral traditions are not unrelated
and do not occur in a vacuum. I am insisting on a perspective that
allows us to create new ways of seeing data. One can best do that
by boldly adapting an Afrocentric openness to a method grounded
in seeking location. Disparate pieces of information are only seen
as such when we are unable to see the disciplinary idea in the
method of analysis. The questions posed by the prehistory/history
debate are reoriented and located properly when we look through
disciplinary eyes.

Brodkey provides a solid description of a discipline when she
writes

A discipline can be thought of as a commitment to a
specified methodology, a particular way of looking at
material. Thus when disciplinarians write, they display a

particular method. Those readers who share the writer's commitment will judge the article or book as an exemplar of the method. Much of the work of the reader, then, is to ensure that the writer renders the method properly. Needless to say, reading and writing are similarly conceptualized, since both activities focus on the degree to which a method has been realized. When this is the case, it is possible to see articles and books as interesting examples of a method. Imagine all the works exemplifying a particular method as beads on a string. Each bead can be judged independently because it is being judged as a bead. With the attention going to the "beadiness" of each and every bead as a bead, the essence of the collection seems to inhere in the merits of individual beads.[151]

The argument I have made is that Africalogy is a discipline because it is a commitment to a way of looking at phenomena. Brodkey is also clear in her understanding of the difference between a discipline and interdisciplinary study.

Interdisciplinary study is not primarily a commitment to a method, but to a topic. Consequently, in interdisciplinary studies, a particular axiology rather than a method links one text to another. Needless to say, then, texts are related to one another as beads in a necklace, rather than as beads on a string. This being the case, textuality is less a matter of individual beads and more a matter of the relationship between the beads and the necklace.[152]

In both principle and practice, particularly so if the practice is good, the researcher is implicated in his or her work. Brodkey says that "all scholarship recognizes that researchers are implicated in their own research."[153] In this way the Afrocentrist seeks to abandon ethnocentric and racist systems of logic and, therefore, to place the undiscussed in the center of discourse. We cannot be committed to any of the so-called "traditional" disciplines and prosecute Africalogy as discipline. History becomes only one of the many building blocks essential to the full explication of phenomena. The same holds true for psychology or communication or sociology. Therefore, the prehistory/history question accquires a different kind of countenance and the Afrocentric scholar locates the issues roundly in Africalogical inquiry.

Africalogy is a separate and distinct field of study from any of the composite sums of its initial founding disciplines. While historians, communicationists, political scientists, psychologists, dance/theater scholars, literary critics and others with Afrocentric perspectives on phenomena, events and persons came together in the creation of departments and programs, they no longer remain merely historians, communicationists, political scientists, psychologists, dance/theater scholars, literary critics. They represent the first stage of the intellectual crystallization of the field that could only be complete with the establishment of a research degree to train scholars in the perspective and methods of the new field. Such scholars, contemporary Imhoteps, benefit from the coalescing of a discipline; they, in turn, institutionalize their broad training, within the bounds of Afrocentric understanding. In effect, and with few exceptions, this is how all fields and disciplines arise.

What this means, of course, is that journals must reflect the new scholarship. Africalogists cannot be judged as communicationists or historians, they must be judged as Africalogists. Research reported in our journals must be evaluated on how well it reflects reality not the degree to which it employs the traditional Eurocentric frame of reference. To impose on our scholarship the very frames the establishment of the discipline questions in terms of perspective is to uphold once again the Eurocentric method that cannot refrain from seeking, as Richards has said, to fill all the spaces.[154] Furthermore, this process sets the bases for judging failure. By virtue of its effort to break open the restraining walls of a provincialism, Afrocentricity repudiates the imprisonment of knowledge while not repudiating the right of Europe to view the world from its cultural center. It must not, however, be permitted to impose that view as universal. The evaluation of the Afrocentric enterprise must be carried out in congruence with the demands of the discipline in relationship to the centrality of the African historical experience. What is required of Europeans and European Americans is a degree of humility, an attitude that has been appropriate but rudely and often arrogantly (the whole history of the British and French campaigns in Africa and Asia; America's Philippine, Native American, and African oppression, Italy's invasion of Ethiopia, etc.) rejected in white political circles. The community of peoples requires of us all submission to the sovereignty of us all, taken abstractly as the spirit of humanity and taken concretely as our responsibility to every other human being. 冽

African Languages

There are at least 1,000 separate and distinct languages in Africa, making it the most linguistically complex continent. Yet no more than thirty African languages have more than one million speakers, only five languages have more than 20 million speakers. Therefore, on a continent where the majority of people speak at least two languages and some even as many as six, the development of new trade and commerce languages has created various pidgins, Krio, Pidgin English, Kituba, in addition to the widely accepted lingua francas such as Swahili, Lingala, Fanagolo, Sango, and Arabic. The colonial languages of English, French, Italian, and Portuguese are also widely used by the elites.

The first attempts by Europeans to classify African languages were based on their structural myths about Africa. Consequently, they gave names to a basic classificatory scheme that emerged from their frame of reference with Europe at the top of a hierarchy where Africans were at the bottom. Such irrational ideology unfortunately governed their classifications.

Sigismund Koelle collected word lists for 150 West African languages in 1854 from his base in Freetown, Sierra Leone, and derived eleven language groups. About forty languages were beyond his ability to classify. He could not place them in his scheme at all. Only a couple of groups exceeded fifteen languages. Nevertheless, Koelle is generally credited with laying the basis for Western linguists to see the Mande as a language family.

Wilhelm Bleek, in 1862, tried to demonstrate the unity of the Bantu language family. He coined the term "Bantu" for his classification meaning "the people" in most languages. As Bleek was doing with "Bantu" so the French linguist, Ernest Renan, was trying to do in East Africa. Renan coined the terms "Hamitic" and

"Cushitic" to refer to Ancient Egyptian, Amharic, Galla, Somali, Beja, Berber to suggest that these languages related to Ham or one of his descendants much as had been postulated that the Semitic languages and people were the biblical descendants of Shem, according to an interpretation of the Genesis biblical account.

Already this account was ethnocentric and chauvinist in its application of a particular cultural classification to African languages based on a sacred book not generally accepted in the African cultures. Moreover, these classifications were to cause constant arguments between Eurocentric linguists as they attempted to further establish a uniquely "negro" language of Africa. What they were finding was connection between African languages and whereas Koelle had come up with eleven groupings, linguists were seeing a smaller number of groups. Another problem was that the French linguists and the German linguist, using their own languages, did not often agree on what to call the various classification groupings. The French, for example, can use "noir," "negro," "Africain," or "negre" to refer to a black person, depending on shade of meaning. German does not possess the same flexibility, though both languages have created colorful pejoratives.

Common Classifications

The two earliest Europeans to attempt overall classification of African languages were Friedrich Mueller in 1876-88 and Karl Richard Lepsius in 1880. They laid the basis for the racist thinking which predominated in language classifications for nearly one hundred years after them. Mueller, an Austrian linguist, worked out a classification of the world's languages based on a correlation of hair type and languages. In Africa, Mueller's division was as follows:

Tufted-Haired People Languages

Bushman-Hottentot
New Guineans (Pacific)

Fleece-Haired People Languages

Negro
Bantu

Wavy-Haired People Languages

Hamitic
Semitic
Nuba-Fulah

Such a classificatory scheme for languages would certainly not stand for long and it was not without its competition, though as we know too well such schemes based on racial ideology consumed most areas of German and indeed European sciences for decades.

Lepsius proposed a language classification scheme involving three major divisions:

1. *Semitic*

    Arabic

2. *Hamitic*

    Hausa, Berber, Fulani, Masai, Bari

3. *Negro*

    Bantu
    Mixed Negro

The preceding classification scheme exists with the inclusion of Carl Meinhof's correctives to Lepsius' barebones scheme. For example, Meinhof added Fulani, Masai, and Bari to Lepsius' Hamitic group. Dietrich Westermann, on the other hand, proposed an alternative which consisted of these groups: (1) Bantu, (2) Hamitic, and (3) Sudanic. Westermann wanted to call all non-Bantu and non-Hamitic languages Sudanic. He linked the Khoisan to Sudanic and the Semitic to Hamitic.

Maurice DelaFosse and Lilias Homburger restricted Hamitic to Ancient Egypt, the Berber languages, Berber, and the Ethiopian languages. They created a class of languages which they called Negro-African or Sudano-Guinean.

The most widely accepted classification is the one proposed by Joseph Greenberg. He consolidated all of the languages of Africa into four classes: (1) Niger-Kordofanian, (2) Nilo-Saharan, (3) Khoisan, and (4) Afro-Asiatic. Although Greenberg's classification has been debated by European scholars such as Istvan Fodor and Malcolm Guthrie on the issue of genetic relationship of languages, it is the critique of Cheikh Anta Diop and Theophile Obenga which raises the more profound questions. While Fodor and Guthrie suggest that genetic relationship of languages can only be discovered in regular phonological correspondences among them and Greenberg's supporters argue that similarities in sound and meaning in numerous instances of body parts, grammatical elements, natural phenomena and lower numbers cannot be ignored, Obenga and especially Diop contend that Greenberg does not go far enough. They suggest the unity of African languages, the genetic relationship of all African languages based on the pharaonic languages. And so we have the basis of the first Afrocentric approach to language classification in Africa.

The Cultural Question and the Problem of Critique

There is a solid intellectual tradition of value issues being placed in the context of culture. Within the Western social sciences, anthropology, communication, sociology, and psychology, a growing corpus on culture has produced more than one hundred definitions of culture.

The Afrocentric scholar Maulana Karenga has argued for two types of culture: popular culture and national culture.[155] He distinguishes between these types of culture in this manner:

> Kawaida maintains that it is the fact that Blacks have a *popular culture* rather than a *national culture* which stands at the heart of the cultural crisis they suffer. The problem of popular culture begins to become clear by its very definition.
>
> Popular culture, Kawaida posits, is the unconscious, fluid reaction to everyday life and environment. In other

words, it is social thought and practice defined and limited by its unconsciousness, fluidity and reactiveness.

By contrast, *national culture is the self-conscious, collective thought and practice thru which a people creates itself, celebrates itself and introduces itself to history and humanity.*[156]

Karenga is useful and heuristic in regards to culture and his work leads directly to the possibility of raising epistemological questions of the idea of culture as philosophical culture, social culture and material culture. I take philosophical culture to include the presuppositions, proverbs, myths epics and propositions that form an ideological position. Social culture relates to the political and behavioral aspects of a human group. Material culture refers to the objects, concrete, iconic, symbolic, and conceptual that constitute the visible, physical or cognitive aspects of the group. A human group or society serves as the base of cultural creation but as Preiswerk and Perrot say:

> Culture is not to be confused with society, the human group from which it emanates, and which it characterizes. Whereas society is linked to a certain area, except for collective migration, culture can "travel," can be exported. Cultural encounters are a permanent phenomenon in history, be it through war or conquest, or by means of peaceful communication. Whoever leaves his "cultural area" (missionary, explorer, businessman, teacher) can take on the role of an agent, modifying the encountered culture as well as his own, once reintegrated.[157]

Culture exists in all of as we are all a part of some culture and cannot during our lifetime divest ourselves of culture we possess various "cultural" identities, some more than other because of the complexity of their historical situation. One may be at the same time, a Yoruba, Nigerian, West African, and African.

Charshee McIntyre has raised some interesting cultural questions about African Americans who are products of mixed gene pools, particularly African/European and African/Native American mixtures. She has extended her discussion to South Africans called "Cape Coloreds."[158] One must be careful not to confuse the transmission of culture with the biological transmission of genes. Yet, it is clear that cultural factors influence racial affiliation in the case of persons of mixed biological origins. If an African of mixed gene pool origin adopts European speech, dress, and terms of protocol he or she will be considered European or more European than African. On the other hand, the choice of an African language, African dress styles, and customs will cause the person to be considered African.

Race does not determine culture but because of the "proximity factor" it figures in the formation of certain cultural attributes much like age, another biological factor, conditions certain cultural behaviors. Race functions as a sort of subset of culture in some regard. As a scientific term, however, it lacks validity except in the sense of gene-pools.

A few years ago Joyce A. Joyce, a brilliant critic and theorist, proposed in an essay that Henry Gates, Jr. and others had "denied blackness or race as an important element of literary analysis." She was roundly attacked in a white literary journal, *New Literary History*, by Gates and Houston Baker, Jr. The viciousness with which she was attacked and the prominence of her attackers in the field of literature caused consternation among numerous African American intellectuals. Certainly Joyce's position could have been strengthened by reference to history but nothing in her essay seemed to justify the vehemence of the attack upon her.

Joyce argued that consciousness is predetermined by culture and color, meaning essentially that how and what one writes are functions of the social, cultural, political, and racial context in which they live. She argued consistently and with great cogency that there was a contradiction in the values postmodernists or post-structuralists or deconstructionists seek to transmit and what readers or the masses expect. Anyone familiar with the African American community could see this immediately. Her intention was to criticize those who sought to join some mythical white "mainstream" by denying the significance of culture on writers and readers. Both Gates and Baker attempted to belittle Joyce's criticism, employing the most vile forms of Eurocentric argumentation.

Gates wrote "it is probably true that critics of Afro-American literature (which, by the way, I employ as a less ethnocentric designation than 'the Black Critic') are more concerned with the complex relation between literature and literary theory than we have ever been before." (349) But he missed the point of Joyce's argument and introduced another level of confusion. Critics of Afro-American literature and Black Critics are two different things and neither is necessarily ethnocentric. Furthermore, Joyce's idea that the African American writer must write for the people, in language that the people can understand, is most appropriate. Gates in reply to this point argues that teachers ought to be interpreters for the masses of the people. In his response he revealed a fundamental belief in the inability of the people to understand for themselves. If literature is to be judged effective, then it must be judged to have some impact on the lives of people. People must understand it. The meaning of literature for the masses must be the enriching and empowering of people; it cannot mean that we befuddle the masses. There is nothing wrong with straight talking and straight writing. Good literature has always been accessible to the people; this has been our most enduring legacy as writers.

Houston Baker's response to Joyce is even more troubling than Gates' inasmuch as Baker seems to recognize the contradictions inherent in his attack on Joyce in the same literary journal that he labels, probably correctly so, devoted to "Euro-American points of view." Baker believes that Joyce misunderstands the nature of contemporary society and seeks to establish his position by suggesting that "life has become more complex in a decade of rabid conservatism, reduced material resources, actual starvation, and religiously inspired bigotry." This is an excellent try at making a platform for launching an attack on Joyce's central point: African American writers ought to write in ways that can be understood by the masses. However, the platform is flawed because one could argue that life has not become that much more complex in ten years. Quite frankly, all of the characteristics of life mentioned by Baker appeared in the 1960s and are with us in the 1990s. Anyway, if life had become so much more complex, then it would have been even better for us to become clearer as writers and critics.

The real issue is whether or not African American critics will run after European critics or establish their own critical instruments. The debate in the literary criticism arena has implications for those of us in other fields to the degree that the lack of clarity among our critics means that we will continue to be judged and evaluated by the theories and methods which emerge out of a white bourgeois racial supremacist universalist ideology contrary to either our culture or condition. No matter how you do it, you cannot justify a position that says Derrida, Althusser, Lacan, and Baudrillard are somehow in harmony with the "freedom cries" of the millions of Africans in South Africa. Baker seems to be suggesting that there is something in these deconstructionists and post-structuralists that is similar to the revolutionary spirit in South Africa; the two situations have nothing in common.

The so-called decentered operations of reason are based on Eurocentric cultural assumptions. Two elements of those assumptions are (1) valorization of Europe at all times and (2) hostility to others. Indeed, Preiswerk and Perrot see the search for decentration as elusive because of valorization of Europe based on Eurocentric notions or reason and science.

When Westerners studying a different culture believe they are rooted in reason and science, it does not necessarily follow that they achieve decentration. An epistemological position which limits itself to urging the adherence of the researchers to a code of scientific behavior and to a comparison of the results with those obtained by other researchers is, in our opinion, insufficient. In the intercultural context, particular care must be taken not only to eliminate distortions stemming from the researcher taken as an individual subject, but equally to measure the impact of the social origin of the researcher's knowledge. When four researchers confirm the results obtained by a fifth, this agreement does not necessarily mean decentration, when the five belong to the same culture.[159]

Preiswerk and Perrot are correct because they see that the primary results of the "code of scientific behavior" is to insure similarity of results among researchers of the same culture. It is the choreography, not the number of dancers in the piece, that determines the results.

But clearly reason and science are not the monopoly of Europeans. My intention in criticizing this view is to redirect attention to the transformation of the ideology of science rather than to undermine it.

The Afrocentric critique demonstrates that Eurocentric research advances in three directions: (1) the conferring of negative or positive qualities on others and the manner in which others are evaluated by criteria and measures promoted by one's own in-group; (2) the interpretation of one's own position as reasonable; and (3) the denigration of the other's position by refusing to recognize its existence.

Preiswerk and Perrot call the first mechanism projection and suggest that it is of major importance in the imposition of Western particularism as universal.

> ... there is projection, upon cultures other than Western, of a system of values common to the whole of the Western world. Thus, for example, in their relations with African, Asian and Indian American cultures, Westerners, whether representative of a free market economy or of a planned economy, act on the basis of fairly similar conceptions of time, work, productivity, the importance of material goods, relations with nature, family structure, the role of the young and the old in society, the relative importance of cities and countryside, etc.[160]

It is this problem that constitutes the need for transforming Western education particularly when it concerns other people. Projection conceals diversity and imposes an epistemological perspective contrary to the unique attributes of other people.

There is also rationalization. This occurs in the literature when the European writer assumes that his or her position is the only reasonable one. Such a position fractures communication and imposes a particularism as universal. Denigration represents symbolic and consequently intellectual refusal to recognize the other. In such a methodological world the other remains invisible, not important, concealed, and irrelevant.

The scholar must be keen to these stratagems. When they appear we know that a Eurocentric perspective is likely. Mere presence of these stratagems does not indicate Eurocentrism however. The use of these stratagems is often the result of a Eurocentric outlook which obscures the diverse visions of the world. A self-relevant research project must not utilize clearly ethnocentric and male perspectives as if they constitute the total human reality.

A research project involves the researcher as the principal source gatherer. A decisive impact on the direction of the research project is always provided by the orientation of the researcher whose ambition and status are intimately connected to any project. The sum total of a researcher's intellectual projects represents in some ways an autobiography of the researcher. For example,

> A political scientist who decides on a field study outside his own culture or nation can be motivated by one or another of the following considerations: desire to prove the universality of his theory (or on the contrary, to prove the authenticity of "political cultures"), to follow a fashion, to adapt himself to changes in the foreign policy of his country, to conform to the rules of the foundation which supplies his research funds, to take advantage of his contacts in the political circles of certain countries, to consolidate his position at his university through international activities, to apply his linguistic skills or those of his collaborators, to avoid countries particularly grim from the point of view of living conditions and climate, etc.[161]

What the Afrocentric scholar seeks to avoid is "field projection," that is, the belief that one's traditional discipline contains all of the tools necessary for the analysis of phenomena. If a scholar assumes this type of burden he or she falls headlong into the intellectual chasm Afrocentrism critiques in Eurocentrism; the only difference being that instead of an ethnic group being projected as all encompassing, all-knowing, universal it is a particular field of study that is so projected. The Afrocentrist trained as a psychologist must see the relevance of historical methods in some areas as the historian must see the relevance of artistic and political analysis in others.

The Problem of "Problems"

One of the interesting aspects of the Eurocentric research paradigm even when participated in by African or Asian scholars is the concept of problems, as in people who are "problems." Thus, one finds references to "The Indian Problem," "The Black Problem," "The Mexican Problem," or "The Chinese Problem." Configuring the political, economic, and cultural situation like this, one does not see the overpowering reality that all "problems" have more than one participant. In other words, if there is a problem there is a "White-Indian Problem" or "a White problem with Indians" or "a Black problem for Whites or White problem for Blacks." But to study "problems" this way suggests a reorientation of research so that we raise questions of dependence, domestically and internationally.[162] If we do this we introduce another level of inquiry that reaches the heart of the Eurocentric concern with place and status. That is why, of the Eurocentrists, only the Marxists have raised such questions of domination and class. They have not raised it in reference to European culture itself and consequently remain safely behind the facade of the universality of their cultural position. One of the greatest disappointments with the Marxists is that they cannot step beyond Europe as universal symbol for standards for analysis.

Most of our problems are solved through the use of functional concepts. They assist us in organizing, selecting, classifying, and defining objects. The Afrocentric scholar examines reality by structuring it on the basis of philosophical and functional concepts. As we interact with facts concepts emerge, not in a miraculous manner, but out of the interaction between the scholar and knowledge. Preiswerk and Perrot speak of monocultural, intercultural, and cosmocultural concepts referring to those which serve one culture, several cultures, and all cultures, respectively.[163]

What we discover is that an African concept is often different from the European or Asian concept even though the same term may be used. Take the example of the term "son."

> The concept "son" seems, on first sight, inevitably to be the same in all societies. In reality, ideas on this matter can vary. Vincent Guerry reports the following incident: "Meeting a Baoule, accompanied by a child, I ask him: 'Is it your son?' He answers: 'Yes, it's my son.' To avoid confusion I demand further: 'Is it your real son? Is it the son from your belly?' He says: 'No.' Here I declare: 'Therefore it's not your son.' He replies: 'It's not the son from my belly, but it's my real son.'"
>
> Clearly the categories do not coincide. For the Frenchman there is a fundamental difference between an adopted son and a "real" son. For the Baoule, a member of the family automatically succeeds the deceased father and becomes the "real" father, in no way conceptualized separately from the "physical" father. There are neither adopted sons nor orphans.[164]

As we know one can give numerous examples of the fallacy of transferring concepts from one culture to another without accounting for difference. Preiswerk and Perrot say

> In Western societies, orphans are children who have lost a father, a mother, or both parents. An anthropologist seeking to determine the number of "orphans" in an African society will doubtless come across individuals whose situations correspond to this state of affairs. And yet, the society under study does not necessarily know the term orphan, for according to African tradition the juridical status as well as the psychological condition of an "orphan" do not correspond to those of Europe. There is therefore no reason to distinguish an "orphan" from other children, nor to create orphanages.[165]

When an American or European say that Africans have no concept of time actually they mean that the people have no concept of time in the European sense of lineal, chronological time. It is incorrect to say that Africans have no concept of time; the concept of time is well developed among Africans. If they did not have a concept of time then planting, harvesting, and festivals would be erratic and without organization in African society. Since African societies are highly structured in terms of regularized rites, festivals, and agricultural behaviors, time is an important concept to Africans and the calendar is an African invention that dates back to its Nile Valley origins on the continent. Climatic and ecological determinants assist in the assignation of days, weeks, and months to various activities but in no case is the concept of time ignored.

Nonwhite and non-European are concepts which distort the reality of Africans. Europeans often define others by the absence of a phenomenon specific to their culture. This is a self-centered topology where, for example, an economist may speak of market societies and societies without markets or societies with writing and societies without language. This topology describes what a society is not rather than what it is. Thus, "nonwhites" becomes a term without meaning when applied to Africans or Asians. We do not say robins and thrashers are "nonsparrows."

Use of nonwhite or non-European places the European in a position by which others are measured as being either-or. But knowledge of the African is limited because we do not have specific reference: he is, in effect, nonsomething which makes him definitionally nothing. Almost no European writer would be so callous as to say that Europeans are non-Africans.

All knowledge is a continuation, acted upon by numerous scholars in the quest for some portion of truth. Although we might assume that there are many versions of an event, in reality they are extenuations and attenuations of the same knowledge. No knowledge remains the same and as soon as it is written or spoken it becomes the foundation for future knowledge. One only has to look at the vicissitudes of history to see how ideas have gone through transition depending upon the era and the scholar. When nationalism is important the historians emphasize patriotism; the Marxists highlight class distinctions; and moralists see corruption everywhere. Preiswerk and Perrot are alarmed that one finds the Eurocentric researcher "in pseudoscientific guise, at the service of cultural domination, if not helping to legitimize ethnocide."[166]

Western writers often use Western criteria as standards by which other peoples are to be evaluated. The idea is that African cultures are to "evolve" in the direction of the West in order to be considered civilized. Thus, the African culture cannot be different because if it is, one assumes that it is anachronistic. Westerners seek to dictate the criteria by which other people are evaluated.

The concept "modernization" is problematic on several levels. Often it is used to mean "Westernization" of African economics, although this is not implied in the term. What is implied, however, is evolutionist thinking which gives the western scholar another criterion for measuring Africans' progress. Indeed,

> ... experts amuse themselves in measuring "psychological modernization" among Africans by using the following criteria: modern conception of time, placing the accent on the future; a positive attitude toward government activities; a sense of optimism and control over one's destiny; patriotism; belief in determinism and scientific knowledge; a trusting conception of people; a positive attitude toward the leaders of the country, and de-emphasis of traditional beliefs.[167]

Again the aim is to force Western criteria on African societies. Furthermore, the assumption that these criteria are not possible or probable in Africa means that the researchers have projected an image of African that often does not have basis in fact. It is much like the illusion of the "negro" discussed elsewhere in this book.

Moreover, the idea of modernization is self-topological anyway, suggesting that Africans should become like Westerners. Conceivably Europeans might have something to learn about modernization from Africans!

"Sciencing"

In the United States, for example, a number of communicationists have worked on the discourse style of African Americans in an effort to reveal the fundamental African orientation of that style.[167] What they have shown both lexically and syntactically has been the African base of much of our language. Notions of word play, signifying, the dozens, riddles, proverbs, and sciencing are related to the search for harmony—the flight towards cosmic union often referred to as mysticism. Sciencing is particularly interesting.

Sciencing is the interpretation of a word by using its contemporary constituents as clues to its political and cultural meaning. According to the scholar Maulana Karenga, sciencing grew out of the rhetorical motif of the Moorish Science Temple, an urban-based nationalist religion with origins in 1914.

As a popular analytical instrument among religious and cultural orators, sciencing has a strong tradition in political rhetoric. The African American speaker who uses sciencing is on familiar ground and can find sympathetic audiences.

SCIENCING TERMS

history	-	his-story
negro	-	knee-grow
solar	-	soul-ra
justice	-	just-us
community	-	come unity
imagination	-	image of a nation
America	-	A mir-a-cle
Africa	-	Af-ra-ka
disco	-	disk company
chemistry	-	khem is thee
Israel	-	Ra is God
Research	-	search again

In sciencing each of these terms become useful to the person making an analysis of the political condition of African Americans.

Africalogy cannot escape a concern with sciencing as a functional aspect of discourse because it is out of the elementary uses of sciencing that the communication is able to achieve a greater degree of knowledge. I recall the first time I heard as discourse on Columbus "discovering" America. It was a lecture given on the corner in Harlem in the 1960s. The speaker explained that instead of revealing anything about the Native Americans, Columbus "covered" their history and what we needed to do was to "uncover" this "covering" called "discovery." Quite frankly, the logic of the street-talker was not Aristotelian but it was real, fleshy, truth to us. The evidence that "sciencing" may have had an impact on the discussion in the public on this subject is clear to many African Americans. The argument is more "sophisticated" now but no more correct. Let us review the situation.

Numerous Western textbooks are filled with the idea of geographical discovery of African or Asian or American lands. One can find instances where a writer says Mungo Park "discovered" the Niger River or Columbus "discovered" America. In both of these cases two points are significant. The first is that ethnocentrism is clearly present when the writer assumes that a European "discovered" a place where other people already lived. This ethnocentrism leads to the next point which is an emphasis on the lack of historicity of the indigenous people. Selection of facts becomes a series of judgments claiming to be facts but in reality are accepted opinions. Indeed, epistemologically, what has been presented as an "objective" fact reveals itself as a value judgment, which implies the intrinsic superiority of one mode over another. It is not a question here of knowing whether there is real superiority or not, but to be aware of the valorization inherent in the choice of facts and concepts.[168] The "discovery" phenomenon is widely employed in reference to Europeans in Africa. The names read like the who's who of the National Geographic: Livingston, Speke, Park, Moffat, Stanley, etc.

In reality, the first discoverers and explorers were the people of the East African valleys who discovered mountains, new valleys, rivers, and ways to traverse them. They discovered fauna and flora from place to place and discovered what was edible and what was poisonous. They discovered fresh water lakes and salt water fish. They observed and recorded first the movements of the universe.

Primary discovery, if anything, has to do with the first humans viewing geographical phenomena and passing this information on to others. Thus the first African to see the mountains of the moon, for example, passed that knowledge on to others making it possible for them to record in their minds the location and character of the phenomenon. Therefore, the scholar must be careful in writing about discovery since so much history is laced with a hostility toward Africa. The early European Egyptologists, writing principally in the nineteenth century, were particularly hostile toward Africa. Discovery, even in a sense of civilization, was said to have come from some supposed relationship of Egypt to the Indo-European civilization. Of course, this has been proved grossly inaccurate. But the "move" to subvert Africa's place has been consistent and antagonistic.

Even if we use "discovery" in the sense that it is used when people say "Columbus discovered America" we are employing a positively Eurocentric imposition. It is not even certain that Columbus was the first European to arrive in the Americas. We now know that Africans reached the Americas more than one hundred and fifty years before Columbus. Ivan van Sertima's *They Came Before Columbus* and Michael Bradley's *The Black Discovery of America* show that Africans arrived in the Americas long before it is popularly believed. In the end, our own "sciencing" leads us to the discovery of knowledge.

PART III

EXTERIORS _____

C arter G. Woodson and Asa Hilliard have provided the
Afrocentric paradigm with critical interpretations of what
Western education does to African people. Carter G.
Woodson provides us with a general discussion of the entire
educational enterprise. He is particularly keen in his analysis of
what the received-educational theory of the historically black
colleges teach African American students. Those colleges, like their
white counterparts, are responsible for the miseducation of African
students because they valorize European knowledge but attempt to
devalue African knowledge.

> These "educated" people, however, decry any such
> thing as race consciousness; and in some respects they are
> right. They do not like to hear such expressions as "Negro
> literature," "Negro poetry," "African art," or "thinking
> black"; and, roughly speaking, we must concede that such
> things do not exist. These things did not figure in the
> courses which they pursued in school, and why should
> they? "Aren't we all Americans? Then, whatever is Ameri-
> can is as much the heritage of the Negro as of any other
> group in this country."[1]

He contended that the "seat of the trouble" is in attitudes.

> The "educated Negroes" have the attitude of contempt
> toward their own people because in their own as well as in
> their mixed schools Negroes are taught to admire the

Hebrew, the Greek, the Latin and the Teuton and to despise the African.[2]

In Woodson's mind it was clear that the educational problem, by which he meant the general cultural issue much as Karenga speaks of in his Kawaida theory, was in the enslavement of the African mind.

> The chief difficulty with the education of the Negro is that it has been largely imitation resulting in the enslavement of his mind. Somebody outside of the race has desired to try out on Negroes some experiment which interested him and his coworkers; and Negroes, being objects of charity, have received them cordially and have done what they required. In fact, the keynote in the education of the Negro has been to do what he is told to do. Any Negro who has learned to do this is well prepared to function in the American social order as others would have him.[3]

Furthermore,

> The education of the Negro, then, becomes a perfect device for control from without. Those who purposely promote it have every reason to rejoice, and Negroes themselves exulting champion the cause of the oppressor.[4]

Blacks are "boxed" in an educational framework that creates exiles of revolt and persistent resistance. Woodson feared that the real difficulty in educating black people stemmed from the passing on of white biases.

> Taught from books of the same bias, trained by Caucasians of the same prejudices or by Negroes of enslaved minds, one generation of Negro teachers after another have served for no higher purpose than to do what they are told to do. In other words, a Negro teacher instructing Negro

children is in many respects a white teacher thus engaged, for the program in each case is about the same.[5]

Hilliard's advances in Afrocentric interpretation are made in the identification of strategies for miseducation. Where Woodson gives us a philosophical perspective, Hilliard demonstrates how the educational systems of the West conspire to keep African people ignorant of themselves. He does this by isolating strategies used to distort the realities of African history. I have modified Hilliard's strategies and present them here:

Temporal Tampering:

> The presentation of European facts as if they preceded their African antecedents, e.g., Hippocrates before Imhotep.

Isolated Text:

> Choosing to focus on isolated European incidents as history while ignoring African history, e.g., Livingstone and Stanley in Africa.

Creating Illusions:

> Claiming the existence for something which does not exist, e.g., Negro.

Name-Calling:

> Identifying Africans who defended their lands as "warlike" or calling Khoi-San people "Bushmen" or "Hottentots."

Hilliard's original developments in this area have taken on new vigor by the Temple Afrocentric School. A number of scholars at Temple University in Philadelphia, Pennsylvania, such as Kariamu Welsh-Asante and several graduate students, have collected a list of terms that represent "intellectual deviations" as demonstrated by terminology from the Afrocentric School.

Ellison and the Vision of Invisibility

Ralph Ellison, perhaps more than anyone, took the miseducation of Africans as the basis for a profound novel. What Ellison did with the idea of a people brainwashed by the entire society, even African American institutions, was to show how we had become victims of the society and ourselves.

The Invisible Man was published in 1952 and won a National Book Award.[6] It was the literary equivalent of Harriet Beecher Stowe's Uncle Tom's Cabin in that it served to focus attention on the African presence in America. The novel focuses on an idealistic Southern black man who recognizes the limitations of the social, economic and political he was expected to play, but only after his directness and assertion had destroyed his college career and ultimately jeopardized his life. In New York, where he moved when his Southern experience proved futile he discovered his invisibility, that is, discovered that to whites he is invisible. Even the communists, despite their rhetoric, view him as a token. The situation is pointless—he decides to live underground in a Harlem cellar. Briefly, the Invisible Man is the narrator of the novel but several other characters figure in Ellison's array of witnesses. The Grandfather never appears in the novel but he has left the invisible man with a deathbed riddle that becomes a driving force in the work—a motif of the necessary.

The founder of the college is like Booker T. Washington. He knows how to play on the minds of the Southern whites—their guilt and pride. Dr. Bledsoe is the president of the college and he believes that a black person can only succeed by being a hypocritical liar. If the white man asks how are things? You tell him, "fine," even if you are dying. If the white man says, you seem happy, you say "I am" even though you are crying. Mr. Morton is a white supporter who prides himself on helping blacks but he has no understanding of the history that has produced the black condition. Trueblood is a character who contains all of the pathos and echoes of a trapped black man. He has internalized depression and is guilty of incest. The Vet sees himself as an equal to Mr. Norton and speaks bluntly on many issues. It is the Vet who suggests the values of invisibility to the invisible man. Mr. Emerson, Jr. is son of a Northerner to whom Bledsoe has written one of the traitorous letters. Hating his father, Emerson, Jr., who sees himself as a friend of oppressed people tells the invisible man about the nature of the betrayal. Brockway is an elderly black worker in the Liberty Paint Factory who jealously guards the secret of how makes the paint so white. Mary Jack nurses the invisible man back to health when he is injured at the paint factory. She represents a strong sense of stability. Brother Jack leads the nationalist brotherhood. Ntambno is the advocate and philosopher of the brotherhood. Tod Clifton is a popular leader of the brotherhood and friend to the invisible man. He later becomes a vendor of sambo dolls. Rus is a militant and separatist who resents blacks who associate with whites. Rinehart is a Harlem character whom the reader never meets. He floats in the narrative as a presence never seen.

Finally, there is Brother Tarp and Brother Wrectrum who are members of the Brotherhood. With this host of characters Ellison weaves a mighty novel, an epic of its time. His artistic consciousness is at the peak of his time, his poetic language is forceful and his ability to provide cohesion brilliantly displayed. I think the time focus here is the tragedy of an individual, however, sensitive, to lose out against the demonic forces of a warped society. Ellison highlights the individual against the collectivity—he thrusts the individual plight of the invisible man out front as an element of modernity. In this sense this is a modern novel, written with the sensibilities of a thoroughly modern man: I mean Ellison's symbols are those of the "modern" writer.

My own critique of Ellison is grounded in Afrocentric philosophy. Essentially I contend that the African American writer ought to be centered in his or her culture. To do otherwise is to become marginal, peripheral. This is true, or should be true, for all writers since the American culture is not a completed project and we all have our historical legacies. The reason for this has to do with the overwhelming power of Ellison's symbolic prose. He draws on Sophocles, Homer, Dostoevsky, Freud, Jung, Burke, Eliot, Joyce, and Malraux for the texture on his novel. He combines these images with symbols from Richard Wright, the blues and spirituals, our epic story, and personal experiences. Like jazz riffs, some of these symbols and allusions trail off in a disappearing act—you see them and then you don't; Ellison is in the symbolist tradition of

Melville and Hawthorne and perhaps the more vernacular tradition of Hemingway and Twain.

This is a problem for me, not so much for Ellison, and certainly not for the novel which is, as we have come to accept over the years, a remarkable literary feat. I find the *Invisible Man*, in some senses, a truly African book, a tour de force of the multi-faceted, many-sided, and polyrhythmic nuances of the African way with all of its percussion, syncopation, and energy. I like what Ellison does in this novel with that approach but I don't believe he had the faintest idea that he was using an African form. The only way I can know this is because of the subsequent impressions he has given—the idea that he is simply a writer, that he owes no allegiance to Richard Wright.

On another point, Ellison is brilliant. He shows that the anchor the invisible man has is his own folk traditions; traditions Ellison might want to question himself. One should not try to get away from the magical quality of the folk traditions, they inspire the novel and give it rich texture with themes, images, myths, and symbolisms. The invisible man finds his enlightenment, his truth, as he finds his blackness. His movement up is when he plunges into a dark manhole. The rhyme from the folklore "If you are white, you're alright; if you are brown, stick around; if you are black, get back," appears throughout the novel.

In the end, however, this is not a novel written for black people—it uses the vital images and creative allusions of African people in the U.S. to tell a poignant story to white people. I do not mean that we do not accept its brilliance but it is a distorted, twisted, marginal reality—in the final analysis, though gifted with a style and flair, and capable of mastering the novel as form—Ellison is not writing this novel to me however much he uses my materials. His aim is to write to a white audience, to show them this invisibility of the African—if possible to create thought, guilt, understanding, liberation for the white man.

But the African is invisible because of the hostility toward Africa and Africans. The African disappeared in America, except in the constant Pan African circles of black activists and intellectuals. Ellison speaks about an invisibility caused by the attack on Africa and he does not know it—there is a manner of seeing in this novel that loses sight of the real audience for a writer, his own literary community. But for the African American writer it is confusing because he or she feels compelled to write to the "white" audience. No such constraints are experienced by the white writer who simply writes from a cultural view that is simply natural. Were Ellison to write to a black audience because he knows that this would be his primary reading public he would have quite different experiences.

The invisible man tells his story with a combination of style, irony, and wit. There is also absurdity as he views his trials as adventure. To compensate for his correctability he strings his underground hole with 1,369 light bulbs, gets five phonographs to hear the blues properly, and listens to Louis Armstrong's plaintive "what did I do to be so black and blue." In the end he discovers he is who he is—but that brings to mind the question raised by the African philosopher Frantz Fanon in talking to African people, "who are we?" Fanon saw a profound identity crisis confronting the African as a result of five hundred years of European domination—the wonderful aspect of this novel is that Ellison tries to establish in the mind of his reader the territory that belongs to the African. He chooses the battle royal, the dozens, chitterlings, pig ears, mustard greens, the subway, spirituals, folklores, and blues—above all else this is a blues poem, an expression of a condition, a will to escape, even if that means making yourself invisible by living underground.

By the 1960s and early 1970s the African wanted visibility—assertiveness was the order of the day—Ellison had inadvertently contributed to the possibility of understanding the anger of the black masses. Black power and black is beautiful became common phrases and bonding terms. If black was now beautiful, then the color ought to be worn so others could see it.

Visibility was a rejection of invisibility, a rejection of the back-of-the-bus, a refusal to go along and a return to our historical and ethical center. Indeed, we captured the moral ground, the high ground. Our escape into the subterranean environment of America had denied what we had. So no question could be decided without reference to our struggle. The assault on the American conscience has always been an ethical assault. How can you accumulate trillions of dollars of wealth on the basis of free and extracted labor of Africans working from "can't see in the morning to can't see at night" and not have any semblance of decency around any number of social or academic or economic situations? One hundred million Africans were uprooted in the European slave trade and exported to the Americas. Twenty five million died in ships, in dungeons, or by committing suicide—there never has been a national cleansing of this vast example of international criminal activity—it is this situation that sits at the back of Ellison's novel. The African American came to school with an unusual heritage—having come a great distance in such short time against incredible odds. Remember the slave had no rights, no right to hire self out, to marry, to make contracts, to plan her or his own time and could be punished at will. To make me go away—me as the symbol of the culpability of those who looked for the apotheosis of whiteness in a white supremacist world—I was to disappear—the African had to become invisible—he couldn't be seen—all public places either denied our existence or said we didn't matter, the literature omitted Africans as the idea was to forget. In the process, we have also forgotten but in our forgetfulness we have lost the meaning of our present situation. Our invisibility must never again be assured. For the sake of this nation, the African presence and the meaning of it with all of its nuances must be seen as a peculiarly American response to the European slave trade. The impossibility of our invisibility in culture, art, the sciences, cuisine, history, literature and music is assured by the writers who speak in the tradition of Ellison.

Ellison recognized our flight toward cosmic union as a sort of mysticism, not magic which is entirely different, but mysticism, mediated by myth, narrative myth, working itself out in our collective lives as part of a larger context. The human nature, our nature, must be in harmony with the environment in order to be at peace. Unlike magic which seeks to control nature and the environment demonstrating an avidity for power and mastery, mysticism unites us with the invisible through the visible as we become in an Ellisonian sense whole again.

Tuning to the Cosmos

The ancient Egyptians held that humans reflected the deities and that the best moral position was to be in tune with the cosmos as governed by the deities. Although the classical priests recognize certain unique capabilities of humans they saw humans as part of the same cosmos as animals. A special relationship existed between humans and other animals under the power of the deities. In fact, humans are expected to be in harmony with the forces of the universe. Thus evil and good are not oppositional in human nature but appositional, a reflection of the internal harmony of the universe itself. The ancients were students of nature. And as students of nature they analyzed the conditions of men and women from observable facts.

Therefore, the modern debate as to whether humans are essentially good or evil did not occupy the minds of the classical priests. They were sure that humans possessed both good and evil. If one assumed that humans were essentially good and tried to attribute evils in history to social causes he would be begging the question because humans are truly at the root of most evil tendencies in history. If one assures that man is essentially evil he is questioning in a way that show he is not "essentially" evil because he would not be able to reach such a conclusion if he were. After all the quality of the being that judges himself in such a remarkably direct way is without question one of uniqueness in character.

I shall not go further with the discussion of the classical African views except to point out that anthropocentric attitudes were more extensive among the ancient intellectuals than they are today when we know that neither our planet, sun, nor galaxy is central to the cosmic immensity of the universe.

The Question of Marxism Again

Classical attitudes are discovered in the myths and sayings of African people to the extent that the interconnectedness of humans to ecology, environment, community, and universe reflects the world view of Africa. Afrocentricity contends that human problems become problems when humans no longer appreciate the connectedness to nature. One can follow the path of these problems in

Marxist formulations as well as any. Afrocentric critiques are possible in every sphere and of every ideology.

Marx's revolution in economic thought occurred largely because he reconceptualized the social relations that made possible commodity production in bourgeois capitalist societies. He rejected the idea, advanced by some economists, that crises of economic systems were the results of formal possibilities. Rather he contended that the crises of the economy in capitalist societies were manifestations of all of the contradictions of such societies; in fact, the crises would recur because they were systemic. What is introduced in social relations, therefore, is a markedly materialist project.

In short, the recurrence of the overproduction of capital led to the overproduction of commodities which meant that they could not be sold and therefore produced an economic crisis. This presented a new mode of social relations in the European world. Prior to the capitalist "evolution" crises were produced because of natural constraints such as floods, famine, plagues or war which caused use-value underproduction. The capitalist mode, on the contrary, overproduced exchange-values. In the first situation, that is, in the pre-capitalist mode people produced what they used, under-production of what was necessary for use, whether due to plague or war, meant an economic crisis. In the capitalist system the idea is to produce for exchange-value usually money, and when there is overproduction the system experiences a crisis.

Marx argues that under capitalist economics the material production process is inhibited or constrained from producing use-values because of the pressure to produce exchange-values. What is clear is that in addition to constraints on material production such as nature, labor productivity, and resource scarcity, the capitalist emphasis on production for creation of more exchange-values inevitably leads to a crisis.

The social relations are constrained because material productions of society are separated from the laborer who generates production. In effect, material production becomes value production and this transformation throws the capitalist and laborer into opposition, conflict, because of their relative positions in the production process. What Marx suggests is that a correlation exists between the contradictions inherent in the production imperatives of exchange-value seeking and relations of production as defined by the work of the laborer. Thus, a class division exists between the capitalist and the laborer.

Material production is inseparable from exchange, distribution, and consumption. Marx did not analyze production independent of social relations and institutional parameters in which exchange and distribution occur. Therefore, the material production and social relations must be seen in their totality.

In the end what Marx does is to reintroduce a unity into economic theory as it relates to Europe by showing a historico-genetic relationship of the basic forms that make capitalist production possible. He restores the relationship between the laborer and material production in an explication of capitalist production as a whole and engages in a discussion of the forms of value, commodity, and money. Two points must be made at this juncture.

My critique is not based on a fundamental rejection of Marx's analysis but rather on the inability of Marx to see the interrelationship of culture and economics. Although social relations are central to Marx, by social relations he means essentially economic relations, not cultural relations. To be sure, in one sense all cultural activities are social relations but in an Afrocentric use of the term "culture" I mean the generative expression a people's myths, motifs, and celebration of their history. Economic relations become the results of cultural relations, the most elementary of human expressions, e.g., religion. Afrocentricity totalizes cultural, economic, and social organization, demonstrating the essential character of human society from the centrality of Africa and the primacy of the classical civilizations.

The second point is based on the Marxist's hierarchy of social and economic organization: communist, socialist, capitalist, mercantilist, feudal, communal. What this Darwinistic concept of evolution does is to reserve for the "highest" forms of economic and social organization the white European nations, whether East or West. All of the African systems would be, almost by definition, on the "lowest" step of the hierarchy. This is unacceptable as a way of looking at the world.

Much of Marx's own thinking was based on Hegel and Feuerbach.[7] He particularly used Hegel's philosophical premises but extended his intellectual reach beyond philosophy to include history and economics. In fact, MacIntyre says that while Marx was conscious of the need for a new departure in philosophy he kept returning to Hegel, even despite his differences with Hegel on such issues as the origin of the state and of society and the rationality of the state as expressed in constitutional monarchy. Both Marx and Hegel, however, find their sources in the European examples, which is correct and essential, for European writers.

It is the extension of Hegel's Prussian examples to other parts of the world and Marx's European examples that must be carefully scrutinized. While Prussian despotism is akin to Ugandan despotism or South African despotism, they do have different cultural characters. This much I am sure even the most Eurocentric writers would admit. The one fact exemplified in all of Marx's analysis is that human beings are not resigned to their fate; situations can be changed. In his case, where the exploitation of labor by capital had warped social relations it had to be the workers. In our case, where a distorted Eurocentrism, with its religious transmutations in apartheid and white supremacy, projects a false view of human history and culture, it must be challenged by a progressive disciplined Africalogy.

The need for this severe critique of the Marxist hierarchical categorization of society and societies lies in the European concept of the ascendancy of Europe. Marx obviously was no less a victim of his environment on the conceptual issue. Hegel, of course, was a racist. Marx's own intellectual growth began when he wrote his doctoral thesis on Epicurus' transformation of Democritus' atomic theory as a part of what happened to Greek philosophy after Aristotle. Marx saw that Greek philosophy turned from speculative to practical, from metaphysics to ethics and, of course, his own problem was to turn Hegel's speculative ideal philosophy into concrete practice. I am not troubled by Marx's analysis of capitalist theory. He finds a problem and seeks a solution. The troubling aspect of most Eurocentric research, however, Marx included, is that it fails to consider the origins, the bases of knowledge. There is no indication that Marx ever considered the fact that Greek philosophy is derivative in many respects from Kemetic doctrines of Africa. A closed European intellectual practice has permitted the European to avoid coming to terms with African civilizations that pre-date Greek and Roman civilizations by thousands of years. This is seen in Marx as well.

There is also the continuing cultural question with which Marx finds difficulty. Our answer, both to the cultural and economic questions, draws intrinsic value from an Afrocentric analysis of the cultural and economic questions facing Africans. Therefore, while Marxism's answer to the cultural question may be nonexistent, Africalogical studies demonstrate rather straightforwardly that an Afrocentric response to this issue is based on the caterogal paradigm, loss of terms, a fundamental metaphor for both economic and social explanations of the African position vis-à-vis the Western world. European slave traders moved Africans off of physical terms; missionaries and settlers moved Africans off of religious terms; and capitalists moved Africans off of economic terms. This metaphorical conception of the human, African, reality is clearly at the heart of any reclamation process. To reclaim a centered place in economic, social, or political contexts, the African must first find centering in a cultural and psychological sense. To be moved off of one's terms is to be a victim of aggression, whether physical or mental. The conscious behavior of the African must be one of seeking to return from the margins and to regain terms.

In many respects only Sartre was bold enough to refuse to identify Marxism with the writings of the post-Marxists or with Communism in the Soviet Union. The so-called "black super-Marxists" made no such distinction since a respectable part of their philosophy has always been tied to a rejection of capitalism rather than an acceptance of the freedom. The existential freedom which exists within us to define ourselves, to construct ourselves, and to resolve our problems. This reality exists because we are presently engaged in its fulfillment.

Among the African American socialists John Henrik Clarke stands out as the one proponent of freedom who exercised a judgment or made a decision to see culture as the most relevant aspect of a generative approach to socialism, to freedom with all of its explosive significance.

Clarke's early role as an associate editor of *Freedomways* solid-
ified his socialist credentials while creating an enormous amount of
speculation about his intellectual commitment to Marx. As the
dean of African, nationalist historians, John Henrik Clarke, the
most beloved African American historian of the contemporary era,
influenced an entire generation of younger scholars such as Walter
Rodney, Leonard Jeffries, Ronald Walters, Dona Richards, James
Turner, and Charshee McIntyre. The commitment of these authors
tended to be to the idea of Africa-centeredness rather than to any
dogmatic Marxism. Indeed, Walter Rodney best typifies this
pragmatic socialism in the service of Africa.

The shift in Walter Rodney's intellectual orientation began with
a break in the strict Marxist-Leninist terminology which one sees
in some of his earlier articles. One senses that this development was
the result of his concern with the diaspora question and his close-
ness to the methodological principles found in systematic nationalist as presented in the works of the African Americanists, particularly Stokely Carmichael, Maulana Karenga, Malcolm X, and
others. What is fascinating is that even before his teaching stint at
the University of Dar es Salaam, Rodney had attained a remarkable
relationship to the nationalist position, which although not purely
Afrocentric was within striking distance of the concept. In other
words, Rodney had already absorbed quite a lot of the systematic
nationalist position. In "Grounding With My Brothers," a speech
he gave on many occasions in the United States and the Caribbean,
Rodney maintained a strong nationalist orientation. He was able,
perhaps more than any of his contemporary African-Caribbean
scholar writers, to link his intellectual objectives with the work and
aspirations of Africans in the United States and on the continent of
Africa. Indeed, *How Europe Underdeveloped Africa* was a socialist
analysis with definite systematic nationalist sentiments.[9] But even
so, Rodney did not make the leap to an Afrocentric position. He
provided a solid analytical basis for uncovering how Europe had
disrupted the continent beginning with the slave trade and continuing through colonialism. For Rodney's fundamental insistence on
the Marxist position excluded from the beginning his acceptance of
a truly Afrocentric analysis which would have gone further than
Marx to demonstrate that the African nations had essentially been

moved off of their own economic centers, interests, and were serving the interests of the European metropoles. This is not to say that Rodney would have denied the legitimacy of the Afrocentric analysis; it is simply that he injected the class analysis in such a way that European methods prevented him from making the further leap to the centrality of Africa in interpreting African phenomena.

Yet we see in Rodney's speeches and pamphlets a growing concern for systematic nationalist and Pan-African issues. It is unlikely that a scholar as consistent and persistent as Rodney in his main political and epistemological concerns could have shifted to a more systematic nationalist position in this way had there not already been present in his intellectual position certain assumptions and predispositions favorable towards the methodological opening afforded by systematic nationalism.

Like Rodney, Frantz Fanon was interested in the critique of subjugation and dehumanization. He spoke for Algeria and Martinique, Africa and the Caribbean, about the fear, inferiority complexes, servility, and despair of those who have been oppressed. The inexorable reasonableness of his stance and eloquence of his passion placed the dialectic of racism and counterracism on an irreversible course of conflict. His analysis of the African's response to racist oppression became a major work about colonial neurosis. While Rodney had come to his systematic analysis from the Caribbean and Britain, Fanon came to his position from the Caribbean and France. Both were victims of racism and psychological violence.

Frantz Fanon was on the path to an Afrocentric view of history. Although he understood and grasped Marx and Lenin, he was not a Marxist in any common sense. He did not subscribe to the theory that the working class of Africa was revolutionary. Nor did he believe that the European working class would support Africa. In fact, he even regarded the Western proletariat as unsympathetic to the colonized people of Africa. In taking this position, Fanon articulated the Afrocentric view of Marxism: the impossibility of Marxists to incorporate into their thinking the dimension of white racism. Proletariats of the West enjoyed the benefits, even held their places, at the expense of the colonized workers of Africa and Asia.

Fanon grew up in the Martinique of Aimé Cesaire. Since Martinique was a department of France he volunteered for the French army and served in Europe. Between the years 1945 and 1950 he studied medicine at Lyons and edited for the Black Student Caucus a paper he called the *Tom Tom*. In 1951 Fanon completed his dissertation in medicine and wrote the powerful *Black Skins, White Masks*, which sought to look at the psychological ravages which affected colonized Africans. Fanon's fortune as a result of his analysis was his appointment as the head of psychiatry at Blica-Joinville Hospital in Algeria about the time the Algerian Revolution began. Because he was convinced of the rightness of the Algerian struggle he found himself increasingly in conflict with the French authorities. He assisted the rebels for two years and finally had to resign his post at the hospital. Fanon could not find peace on the sideline of history and so after the First Congress of Black Writers and Artists in Paris in 1956 he decided that he would take up an editorial post on the FLN newspaper *El Moudjahid* in Tunis. This led him to further involvement with African Liberation ideology of which he was to become a principal theorist. Although he begins *Black Skin, White Masks* saying "I am talking of millions of men who have been skillfully injected with fear, inferiority, complexes, trepidation, servility, despair, abasement" by the time of his death at 36 he was speaking *for* millions of Africans—in the Caribbean, in the Americas, and on the continent.[10]

David Caute placed Fanon's political resistance in the intellectual tradition of the charismatic prophet when he wrote "Karl Marx was 'created' by capitalism; Garibaldi by Sicilian poverty; Lenin by the Russian aristocracy; Gandhi by British imperialism; Fanon was created by the white man."[11] This is not correct. Fanon was created by *The Wretched of the Earth* who were victims of white oppression. To say as Caute says that he was "created" by the white man does not say enough. Indeed, the revolutionary impulse in Fanon was directly related to increased knowledge of the conditions of his people. He became a restless revolutionary activist whose militancy had led him to participate in the Algerian Revolution but had reached its full power in his political writings.

Unfortunately, Caute is too busy trying to place Fanon in the Western Marxist tradition to see the essential African response to oppression that he makes. While at thirty-six he had not fully developed an Afrocentric ideology, he was most surely on his way. Caute's misunderstanding of Fanon leads him to the conclusion that Fanon would not have understood Malcolm X or Marcus Garvey. Indeed, everything in Fanon suggests the opposite. Since Fanon's ideological developments were inspired by Cesaire, a vigorous antiracist, his path was the same as the antiracists in the United States. Like other Eurocentric writers, Caute seeks to claim even the contributions of the most significant political philosopher of the 1960s by saying that all Fanon did was in terms of the European revolutionary tradition. Of course, Caute assumes that there is neither another tradition nor another revolutionary people. Both assumptions are wrong.

There is in Fanon a giant step toward the Afrocentric methodology. His work bears an essentialist, abstract character which seeks to strip bare the rhetorical nature of white propaganda. In this sense, Fanon's style is much like the essay style of Baldwin who was a better essayist than novelist. Fanon speaks without ambiguity about "the black," "the white," "bourgeoisie," "colonized," and "peasants."

The Afrocentric method confronts the Eurocentric viewpoint on moral grounds and demonstrates its vacuousness in race relations, the primary field of interaction with others. For whites integration means that the African must become like the whites. Whites also believe that they must accept Africans in order for integration to work. Any Afrocentric analysis must dispense with this position because it is theoretically and intellectually vapid. There is, as James Baldwin noted in *The Fire Next Time*, an impertinence on the part of whites to assume that they must accept Africans.[12] The thought has never occurred to them that the African may not have agreed to accept them.

Fanon found in his assault on colonialism a method for liberating the self. As a political activist Fanon was keenly aware of the individual consciousness was intricately linked to collective consciousness. His training in psychology and psychiatry had prepared him for a psychoanalytic analysis of the African's situation. To understand this situation with all its nuances and complexities it was necessary to study the neurotic structures of individuals.

Fanon did not see the African's quest for psychological and political liberation in following the European. In his view the white man had become the principal producer of destruction. "When I search for Man in the technique and the style of Europe I see only a succession of negations of man, and an avalanche of murders."[13]

Therefore, the Fanonian method of revolution against white colonization is both a rejection of Europe and an act of violence against oppression. This takes a national and activist character in as much as colonization is violence itself; it must be violently rejected. He sees violence as a form of positive, humanistic self-assertion against oppression. It is the self asserting itself as human against an inhumane system. Thus, the lack of will to assert against such a system is tantamount to accepting one's status as victim.

The success of the violent confrontation with colonialism rested on three factors according to Fanon: (1) The will of the colonized people to liberate themselves, (2) the fact that colonies were markets for the oppressor nations and protracted war disputed markets, and (3) the fact that the colonial powers feared the communists would infiltrate the national resistance.[14] He believed that under such conditions the use of violence would succeed. Indeed Jean-Paul Sartre had written in the preface to *The Wretched of the Earth*, "The native cures himself of colonial neurosis by thrusting out the settler through force of arms. When his rage boils over, he rediscovers his lost innocence and he comes to know himself in that he creates himself ... to shoot down a European is to kill two birds with one stone, to destroy the oppressor and the man he oppresses at the same time."[15]

Sartre captures Fanon's essential point in the drive for liberation. In Fanon, method is the internal, centralizing force of the oppressed reaching toward freedom. He writes "at the level of individuals, violence is a cleansing force. It frees the native from his inferiority complex and from his despair and inaction." Since the African is radically dehumanized by the process of colonization his violent action is necessary for psychological liberation. For Fanon, Gandhi's methods were inauthentic forms of decolonization, nonviolence never permitted the oppressed to "win" freedom, and "struggle" must never be confused with violence.

Revolutions are short-term affairs. Human emotions last a long time. Violence that results in the killing of human beings is problematic as a liberating ideology apart from the moment of the action. The liberator may be haunted by the killing for many years. Indeed those who participate in the liberating violence are few in numbers compared with the beneficiaries. How do we go about liberating *their* minds? This is the dilemma of African governments that have seized power politically but have not gained control over the cultural or educational lives of their people. This is different from taking over control of institutions. Unquestionably schools and broadcasting stations can be controlled and governed but what is taught and what is broadcast is as important, perhaps more so than merely governing.

The prosecution of a revolution never touches every individual in a society. And violence is a solitary experience even in collective action. This is not to say that Fanon is totally incorrect in his assessment of the psychological impact of violence on the oppressed. We cannot assume the same situation for those people who are not oppressed. Furthermore, random, non-directed, anarchic individual acts of violence would not be considered either therapeutic or valid in Fanonian terms. My only point is that it does not always happen that the African cures him or herself of psychological dependence on Europe by thrusting out the settler. Sometimes the settler's culture lives deeply within his soul.

Fanon's ideas were grounded in the resistance tradition of African intellectuals. As a socialist, he was, like Malcolm X, an enemy of white racism, capitalist exploitation, and psychological oppression. Fanon found that revolution demanded a critique of domination much like Malcolm would later discover in his analysis of African experience in America. Although Fanon never succeeded as Malcolm was to succeed in identifying the underlying force of exploitation and oppression as white racism, he was clearly writing in the tradition established by Garvey and Du Bois.

Psychological Questions

Fanon could identify psychoanalytical interpretations as the basis for understanding the complex situations affecting the victims of racism. How did the African epidermalize the economic and social inferiority thrust upon her? Fanon maintained a critical posture toward Freud, arguing that "the neurotic structure of an individual is simply the elaboration, the formation, the eruption within the ego, of conflictual clusters arising in part out of the environment and in part out of the purely personal way in which the individual reacts to these influences."[16] In this passage, Fanon demonstrates an appreciation for the Freudian attitude toward the anomalies accompanying those who have been victimized but he finds difficulty in reconciling various psychological traditions with his attempt to synthesize economic and psychological determination. Although both Freud and Jung have some influence on his work, particularly in terms of theories of sublimation, childhood sexuality, and the collective unconscious, he is not a child of their psychology but rather an Afrocentric precursor.

Like Fanon, we recognize the importance of both Sigmund Freud and Carl Jung who are among the most significant contributors to the European language of social sciences. Terms such as repression, id, ego, Oedipus complex, occultism, extrasensory, alchemy, reaction formation, collective unconscious, rationalization, libido, persona, anima, animus, and superego have become intertwined with the everyday western way of thinking.

Freud was to psychology what Einstein was to physics, or Diop was to classical African civilizations. He altered the terms of Western psychological discussion and presented a new vocabulary. Freudian psychology clearly delineated a conception of the person not usually found in African thought. His view of human nature was pessimistic. His idea of the human race was not exceedingly optimistic due to the enormity of social ills that beset the world. Being born into an irrational world Freud believed that humans could only pass on their irrationality. This irrationality, according to Freud, was based in the nature of human personality. The basic systems of the personality are the id, the ego, and the superego. These systems should be in harmony if a person is healthy but because they are often at odds the person must work to adjust them. If they cannot be adjusted the person becomes angry with himself and the world. According to Freud the id provides fulfillment of the pleasure principle. This principle assists the person in eliminating tension or maintaining tension at a constant level. The ego is governed by the reality principle which, according to Freud, meant the postponement of the discharge of energy until the actual object that will satisfy the need has been discovered or created. The ego has to be able to tolerate tension until it can be appropriately discharged. The superego is the judicial branch of the personality. The superego represents the ideal and strives for perfection, not reality nor pleasures. When a person's conscience comes into play then the superego, the moral keeper of the personality, has been activated.

The Afrocentrist finds little in Freudian views with which to be pleased, largely because Freud was uncomplicatedly interested only in the Eurocentric enterprise as universal. Furthermore, as John Henrik Clarke observed, Freud's notion of the relationship of sex problems to sanity could not be validated by the African experience.[17] Perhaps Carl Jung's theories were more akin to those of the Afrocentric school because of Jung's attempt to understand the wholism of the cosmos.

Jung was Freud's premier student but broke with his mentor during the publication of his major book, *Symbols of Transformation*.[18] Eager to pursue his own line of thought, Jung delved into the occult, astrology, and human symbols. He travelled to Africa, visiting Tunis, the Sahara, Kenya, Uganda, Sudan, and Egypt. He learned Swahili in order to perform word-associations with his African colleagues. These experiences and others in Asia and among native Americans in New Mexico, gave him a broad view of human personality not found in Freudian psychology.

What Jung wanted to know was how symbols, language, dreams, and visions, revealed the collective unconscious of the mind. He discovered that the unconscious manifested itself in the occult, dreams, symbolisms, and myths. Because he used whatever sources existed to assist in discovering truth Jung was often considered unique to other scientists. In this respect, his methods were similar to those of the Afrocentrists who insist on using oral sources, symbols, fabrics, linguistics, botany, animal husbandry, and religious icons to establish the truth about a human situation.

The human personality, according to Jung, is shaped by archetypes, the original model after which other things were patterned. He said there were many such archetypes: fire, a ring, God, birth, death, the hero, demon, earth mother, and power, to name a few. Four archetypes are of such importance that Jung devoted great attention to them: persona, anima, animus, shadow, and the self.

The persona enables one to portray a character that is not one's own. It is a mask worn publicly with the idea of presenting a good image.

The anima and animus are the "inward" forces of the psyche as opposed to the "outward" force of the persona. This inward force is called the anima in males and the animus in females.

The shadow contains more of man's basic animal nature than the other archetypes. Jung saw it as the most dangerous of all the archetypes because it is responsible for the best and worst in humans when dealing with those of the same sex.

The self is the organizing principle of the personality. It is like the sun in the solar systems, organizing, unfixing, and supplying the entire system. As the structuring mechanism the self unites all parts of the personality.

Jung's work has implications for Afrocentric inquiry because he shows how we might utilize the traditional thought of African "psychologists" for guidelines to understanding African culture. For example, Jung is no more significant for the Afrocentric scholar than Anokye, called Okomfo Anokye, who lived in Ghana during the seventeenth century. Anokye helped to construct a set of concepts that applied to the spiritual kinship. Thus, okra, sunsum, ntoro, and mogya represent the major components of the individual. The okra is a person's destiny or mission; sunsum is character, genius, morality. Ntoro, from one's father is personality; and mogya is blood which one inherits from his or her mother.

What neither Jung nor Freud nor very many white psychologists deal with is the psychopathology of white racial supremacy itself. The presence of African culture has been so firmly established in the diaspora and on the continent, both as a continuity and a tradition, the need to defend Africa, if it ever existed, does not exist. On the other hand, the need to find explanations for white racial supremacy thinking remains a major task of Africalogists and other scientists.

The valorization of whiteness is profoundly a five-hundred-year-old Eurocentric enterprise. To engage in a discussion about white supremacy is to employ a term used by whites to legitimize white control over others or to speak about the control exercised by whites over others since the 1600s. Both are political uses of the term "white supremacy." Since white supremacy, in a biological sense does not exist, writers who use the term are using a theoretical construct based on economic, social, and political situations enforced by the military power or the threat of violence.

The term "supremacy" does not enter the literature from the African or Asian side but from whites themselves, thus even the critical European scholars were inclined to use the term when debunking it. From a strong psychological base in the minds of Europeans of the seventeenth-nineteenth centuries the idea of European superiority was cultivated and grew into a mature notion of white supremacy by the twentieth century. Three hundred years of steady European domination of the world had given the Europeans a serious psychological problem. Accompanying the political and economic "successes" of colonization was the seeming capitulation of other people's cultures to that of the European. This led Europeans to the belief in the superiority of their culture, history, economic systems, child-rearing practices, communal organization patterns, art, and architecture. The political manifestation of this was the exercise of a vision of white supremacy. Even the most "progressive" and ethical circles in the European intellectual community insisted that Europe was or should be supreme. Drunk with the intoxicant of racial supremacy the European ethos, as seen in the literature and social relations, exhibited an intense racial psychosis.

Frank Tucker's important essay on *The White Conscience*, written in 1968 but little reviewed and pretty much dismissed by the scholarly public, remains one of the few serious historical attempts in America at the critique of the European domination of the world for the last five hundred years.[19] Tucker's documentary

account of the history of the West shows how Europeans dehumanized themselves and distorted their own values by exercising
brutality against "people of color."[20] Indeed, J. J. Ingalls had said
in a speech to the United States Senate in 1890 that "the race to
which we belong is the most arrogant and rapacious, the most
exclusive and indomitable in history. It is the conquering and the
unconquerable race, through which alone man has taken possession
of the physical and moral world. All other races have been its
enemies or its victims." Nearly a hundred years later the Canadian
scholar Michael Bradley could write that the white race is most
responsible for the pollution of the atmosphere, the great catastrophes of the earth in war, and most of human suffering caused by
racial discrimination.

Even in the debate over the humanity of others, the Eurocentric
view shows an arrogance towards others. When Montezinos
denounced the Spaniards' treatment of the Indians in 1512 he had
one major convert to his position, Bartholeme de Las Casas, later
the Bishop of Chiapas, who was to take up the case of the humanity of the Indians. Sepulveda and Oviedo, two theoreticians of the
Conquistadores, argued that the Indians did not have nationality
and were by nature slaves.[21] But the Indians neither questioned
their nor the whites humanity. That they were different goes
without saying but that hardly constituted a case for questioning
humanity. In this regard the European notion of who was and was
not a human was a self-serving definition.

Las Casas and Alonzo de la Vera Cruz argued that the Spaniards were taking Indians' lands and reducing them to slaves.
Indeed Hanke reports that Las Casas even thought the Indians
could make better Christians than the Europeans.[22] Almost all of
these early European race theorists took it for granted that "the
original man" was white and degenerated to become Africans and
Indians. Rebecca Cann's work has now shown that, if anything, the
mother of those of us living today was a "black woman."

In a far-reaching laboratory experiment with mitochondrial
DNA samples drawn from one hundred and forty eight individuals
from around the world, Cann demonstrated that structurally all
living human beings are descendants of one woman who lived in
Africa about 200,000 years ago. Indeed, Cann and her colleagues

substantiated the fossil work of the anthropologists such as the Leakeys and others. Africalogists like Diop, Ben Jochannan and Obenga had concluded the African origin of civilization through signs and symbols of primordial human beings as well as the legacies of science and philosophy found in the Nile Valley. Rebecca Cann's work gave a biological interpretation of human family-hood. In view of this work it is logical to assume that we are all African.

Establishing African origins should not lead to an inevitable biological determinist line which argues that nature is never modified by the environment. Apart from African origins, however, some scientists have contended that the genes are responsible for all human behavior and culture. Indeed, this line of thinking takes Darwinism to a new level.

The Sociobiologist Project in Culture

As an extension of the biological determinist line, sociobiology declares that "the genes hold culture on a leash."[23] Edward Wilson, the "father" of sociobiology, argues that every aspect of our behavior is directed by our genetic endowment. Wilson's view that natural selection, artificial selection, and sexual selection are the principal pathways to genetic endowment has influenced almost all of the sociobiologist. Rosenberg's *Sociobiology and the Preemption of Social Science* raised profound questions for the study of human behavior in the traditional framework.[24]

What has become most important in the articulation of the sociobiology project is the evolutionary, and by that I mean, Darwinist construction of human emotions, ethics, impulse, problem-solving, and symbol making. Such a construction might be taken to imply that human beings are not responsible for their behavior. The sociobiologists see the problem in such a construction and posit the "hypertrophy effect" which when combined with the "multiplier effect" permits a small genetic trait to become a major social behavior. Thus, moving from genetically determined behavior to social or cultural behavior is not only possible, there are certain hypotheses that help to explain how it happens. When the genetic trait crosses the "threshold" it becomes social behavior. Of course, as in social science, so in sociobiology, we are discussing "concepts," "theoretical possibilities," "analogies," and "metaphors" that cannot be precisely measured or explained. Whether this "threshold effect" exists or not is not the Afrocentric question but rather what are the implications of a theory that could lead to dominant influences artificially redesigning or engineering genes for political and social purposes.

Other approaches to human emotions and values have been credited with providing different assessments of human achievements. In effect, the progressive Western notion of human rights with its roots in eighteenth century British and French culture dominates the discussion of political freedoms. Sociobiology aside, the idea that human society is ordered according a preset hierarchy appears to be central to the European enterprise. Thus, one sees that the human image, in all of its peculiarly Western formulation, whether as it relates to human rights or to human image, is cast in the shadow of hierarchy.

Re-Examining the Knowledge Question

Arthur Lovejoy's *Great Chain of Being* expertly totalized the Western cosmological concept of human beings.[25] Plato and Aristotle are considered the originators of the Great Chain of Being concept. In *Timaeus* Plato advanced the idea of the Demiurge who is responsible for creating a world outside himself. In the working out of this cosmological framework European writers saw themselves—that is, Europeans—as the highest link in the human chain. This was neither the case with Plato nor with the nascent European culture. To the West prior to the coalescing of Europe in the minds of a few regional writers of the seventeenth century, the ascendancy of this European thought reached its climax in the lectures of Hegel whose views on Africa and human rights fell clearly within the hierarchical ideal of Europe. We are, therefore, under obligation to examine the Western idea of the human image.

Josiah A. M. Cobbah has written in "African Values and the Human Rights Debate: An African Perspective" that even the Western notion of human rights has to be questioned.[26] In his penetrating article, Cobbah contends that the Africans who have written on the issue tend to follow the Western paradigm. These authors are necessarily tied to the popular Western notions they have been taught by their teachers. Thus, "while the increase in the discussion of human rights in Africa is both timely and refreshing, a survey of the literature leaves one with the impression that scholars proceed on the assumption that although traditional concepts on the enhancement of African dignity are present in African culture, African societies have become modernized to a point where a discussion of these traditional concepts has become esoteric, or indeed a pretext by Africans to avoid the hard questions about human rights violations for which the Western world expects convincing answers."[27] Cobbah clearly delineates the problem in the ethical individualism of the Western world by demonstrating that it is tied to notions of benevolence, heroism, and sacrifice rather than to the natural duty not to harm one's fellow. He is explicit that "supererogatory acts" emanate from ethical individualism's idea of charity and goodwill, rather than the African communalism worldview. Thus, the human rights notion of the Western world, based on an Anglo-American construction of ethical individualism, is even different from the view held by a minority of Western scholars in the scholastic tradition.[28] The international advancement of the Western idea in human rights has imposed a European natural rights perspective which denies the right of those in "need for sustenance and society's obligation to satisfy this right." Cobbah's attempt is to posit an Afrocentrist's view on the issue of human rights without resorting to the biological determinist position taken by many with white racial supremacist doctrines. What we see is that race is an illusive idea when it comes to the issue of human rights with its philosophical foundation firmly based in culture.

Several recent scholars have challenged the general methodological line on race taken by liberal and conservative writers. Nascimento, and Omi and Winant have demonstrated the illusive nature of the discussion on race in the literature of the Americas and Europe.[29] Liberals often treat racism as prejudice, Marxists treat it as a subset of class exploitation brought about by mercantile capitalism.

Nascimento in a study of Pan-Africanism and South America chose to examine race as a system of domination, "involving violent imposition upon conquered peoples of alien economic, political, religious, linguistic, social and cultural scientific norms and notions."[30] She makes an exceptional observation when she writes "while international monopoly capital is the operative element of world economic dominion, Eurocentrism and its attendant white supremacism are the operative elements of world psycho-social and cultural domination."[31] In both cases the African person is moved off of his or her economic and psycho-social/cultural grounds. The imposition of monopoly capitalism and the imposition of Eurocentrism are cooperative, neither being determinative in its own right, in the negation of Africa and African people. Therefore, we must see racism as transcending the color of skin and see it as a complex and interlocking psychosocial and economic system of domination. Thus, we have returned to the idea of the loss of terms. Africans are deprived of dignity, history, culture, and respect in such a system.

It is important that a researcher understand the complexity of the system of exploitation. Although a considerable amount of work has been done on the explication of the economic aspect of domination and increasing amounts of work are being written on the psychosocial/cultural factors, few of these works have teased out the intricate nature of racial domination. The Afrocentric scholar should be conscious of the nonracial argument in relationship to institutions. One of the most subtle forms of racism is in the use of terms like objective, neutral, color-blind, and nonracial to refer to openness of the psychosocial/cultural system. But the system is itself structured on the basis of racial stratification and regardless of how "nonracial" in approach caretakers of the system may be at the present time, the system remains an instrument of racial domination. The projection of racism by using apparently nonracial terms represents a new development in the discourse on race.[32] Ronald Walters argues that one of the impulses of imperialism is "to create other systems in its own likeness, not only to serve its economic interests but to reflect its particular brand of political philosophy as right and virtuous by the establishment of similar institutions."[33] Walters could just as well have written of the definitional, theoretical, and methodological institutions which could be created by an invasive psychosocial/cultural hegemony.

The imposing ethic establishes itself as more valuable to even a slave than his own psychological or cultural self. The absolute loss of terms at the level of one's cultural control means that culture itself seeks ways to mask its potency. "Yes" might become "no" and "bad" might become "good." Several works have explored the Eurocentric assertion as it related to the African during the slavery era.

John Blassingame's *The Slave Community*, though flawed in some ways, represents one of the first "historical" studies to use the Eurocentric object as subject. He seeks to empower the enslaved African with a historical voice, thereby asserting the centrality of the African's experience in any discussion of European slavery. For Blassingame, the life experiences of the African as revealed in narratives and autobiographies, were not just worthy of study but were essential to an understanding of the slave systems. In the Preface to his work Blassingame complains that "historians have *deliberately* (italics mine) ignored these sources." His complaint is at the heart of the problem with Eurocentric methods: they usually seek to totalize phenomena in the European experience as if it were universal. While we cannot question the centrality of the European view in matters pertaining strictly to Europe, in those matters where the European culture is involved with the culture of others we must always challenge the imposition of Europe on others. Historians, as they have come to be defined in the West, are profoundly Eurocentric in their enterprise and have been unable to consistently transcend their provincialism even while examining African realities.

Blassingame is an extremely astute observer of the historical record but often he falls victim to the Eurocentrism that affects too many of us Africans educated by whites. He writes of the Native American interaction with the Europeans like this, "Consequently, Europeans in North America either exterminated the *war-like* (italics mine) hunting tribes or worked the simple food gatherers to death."[34] But Blassingame knows that to refer to the Native Americans as "war-like" is incorrect and a misnomer. If anyone was *war-like* it was the Europeans who "exterminated" or "worked the ... [Native Americans] ... to death."

Sterling Stuckey's *Slave Culture* and Vincent Harding's *There is a River* represent two monumental works on the nature of the African's presence in America.[35] In *Slave Culture*, Stuckey demonstrates the intrinsic value of the African's commitment to a centeredness by showing that many African Americans possessed the understanding and acceptance of African culture necessary to maintain dignity and strength in the face of hardships. Harding's book, poetic and lyrical, provides a fresh narrative of the role played by the African in his and her own liberation. Taken alongside the works of Blassingame, Huggins and others, the works of Stuckey and Harding constitute a historical consciousness that will ultimately lead to a new Afrocentric interpretation of African American history.

In Stuckey and Harding we see the spiritual, rhythmic, soulful method assuming the proper place in analysis. It is from these two authors that we learn about the inner workings of the African American mind in song and dance, work and play, religion and science, community and church, industry and theater. They remind us of the ancient rites, the so-called secret societies of Africa, in their efforts to uncover the causes and reasons for African American social and cultural behavior in the United States. What I mean is that they reconstitute our history, making it meaningful in innumerable ways by showing the unity of soul and method. Quite frankly, the pattern for this kind of analysis existed in the "secret societies" themselves; often the principal training schools in early classical and late classical traditional African society.

The ancient African civilizations did not separate religion and philosophy. Indeed the contributions to art, literature and the sciences are directly traceable to the religio-philosophical institutions of the Nile Valley civilizations. Expressions of this unity of religion and philosophy appeared in the construction of the temples, memorials, obelisks, causeways, and pyramids of the classical period. The finest works of architecture were based on the principles derived from ancient wisdom which dictated proportions and motifs based on the laws of harmony.

The Greeks called the classical African wisdom mysteries; the modern European writers refer to this wisdom as secret societies. Both designations are problematic. Mysteries is misleading as a descriptive term because one ancient wisdom was only a mystery to the uninitiated. Once a person had learned the religio-philosophical-ethical principles they were not mysteries and consequently should never have been so designated. To call this wisdom "mysteries" is to elevate the Greek conception (as outsiders) of the wisdom as a more important conception than that of the people who created it. In this regard, even the "old scrappers" were often mistaken because they followed the Greek designation.

In Greece itself so-called mystery schools were established and some of them, like the shrine of Eleusis in Attica, contained huge spaces for audiences to see the initiates perform the rituals. The Greeks divided the wisdom into two parts: (1) lesser mysteries and (2) greater mysteries. The lesser mysteries were granted to persons of good moral character who matriculated for the training. Since the lesser mysteries were taught in the form of a pageant, even young children could be admitted. The greater mysteries tested the person in moral, physical, and intellectual areas. One had to be sound in body and mind and show a knowledge of the acquired wisdom before one could successfully pass the test. Once a person passed the test he was a member of the order.

Secret societies is a name given by scholars to the institutions which have inherited and maintained the ancient wisdom. Observing institutions such as the epa, the gelede, the mbira, the poro, the nimba, and the abakua, the European author used the term secret societies to identify them. But these institutions, where the arcana of the shrines, that is, the necessary knowledge for interpretation of sacred symbols and priestly writing, were truly societies of secrets.

An initiate learned the accumulated knowledge of the ancestors and participated in the great drama of "universal" beginning. The vows and obligations of these religio-philosophical institutions laid the foundations for establishing order, justice, peace, and ethics within the various communities.

As Stuckey has shown with brilliant insight into the learning experiences of Africans in America, our knowledge, often accumulated from the ancestors who practiced many of the methods they had learned from their parents and relatives, came from participating in the great narrative dramas of resistance against oppression.[36]

And while "slave" culture was marginal in many ways to the white society, it was not marginal or peripheral in terms of the psychological and cultural caring that took place within the powerful context of Africa-centeredness. Only when scholars wake to the task of examining African lives and events from this position can we fully know what it means to regain our terms.

A slave is one who has been reduced to an artifact of an oppressor's creation and changed into something defined, fabricated, and marked by the will of another as being useful for the oppressor's purposes, thereby losing one's own material and creative terms. Only in this context can we truly understand the dangerous implications of the loss of terms. European slavery maintained the most brutal, total, and repugnant form of human reduction transforming the "organic materiality" of Africans into what was essentially an inorganic violence.

Africalogy seeks to bring a new birth to the intellectual enterprise by encouraging scholarship to tear itself away from the imposition of a European domination, in fact, to place Europe in a normal context, separate from arrogance and within an arena of pluralism without hierarchy. To regain terms, Africalogy must remain free to challenge unquestioned assumptions about the principal issues confronting the African world. Methods must be tied to specific historical and cultural foundations, to the primacy of Kemet, and the foundations most useful are those in which the issues or subjects are centered. An Afrocentric world voice, regaining terms, will be a full, florid, whole, and productive voice, speaking the intellectual ideas of a new, generative category of human inquiry from an African-centered perspective.

Africalogy cannot achieve its purpose as a liberating discipline unless it is founded on assumptions that dignify humans rather than negate them. This dignification of humans begins in a critique but it can never end in critique. Although it is true that when I have waited for a Eurocentric science that liberates humans I have been disappointed, I should have recognized the fundamentally different approach to human knowledge in the Western project. Neither sociology, psychology, political science nor anthropology nor history liberates those who have been victims of cultural, political or economic domination. If anything, the oppressed are victims of the theorists who explain and interpret the condition of the masses in order to be able to more accurately "predict" their responses to an increasing array of stimuli. Africalogists must critique but also in our research we must propose concrete actions that lead to the lessening of disharmony, suffering, misunderstanding, and dislocation.

NOTES

Part I Interiors

1. Cornell West, *Prophetic Fragments*. Trenton: Africa World Press, 1988, p. 270.

2. Trent Schroyer, *The Critique of Domination*. New York: G. Braziller, 1973, p. 15.

3. See Nathan Huggins, *Report to Ford Foundation on Afro-American Studies*. New York: Ford Foundation, 1986.

4. Eric King, "The Employment of Black Males," Second Annual Black Family Conference, Center for the Stabilization of the Black Family, Niagara Falls, New York, October 16, 1988.

5. Robert Plant Armstrong, *Wellspring: On the Myth and Source of Culture*. Berkeley: University of California Press, 1975.

6. Kariamu Welsh-Asante, "Commonalities in African Dance: An Aesthetic Foundation for African Dance" in *African Culture: The Rhythms of Unity* edited by M. Asante and K. W. Asante. Westport: Greenwood Press, 1985.

7. See Linda James Myers, *Understanding the Afrocentric Worldview*. Dubuque, Iowa: Kendall-Hunt, 1988. Myers provides us with a strong interpretation of an Afrocentric worldview.

8. Although I coined the term "Afrology" and used it in *The Afrocentric Idea* to refer to the Afrocentric study of African phenomena, after considerable discussion with my colleagues and students I am now ready to view the term "Africalogy" as a more accessible term. It is more explicit, does not repeat the "Afro" prefix which has generated quite a lot of discussion itself, and is readily understandable by most literate Americans and Africans. Winston Van Horne and Patrick Bellegarde-Smith at the University of Wisconsin-Milwaukee have used "Africology."

9. Abdias do Nascimento, "Pan Africanism and the South American Connection," Du Bois Lecture, Accra, Ghana, August, 1988.

10. Robert F. Heizer (ed.), *Man's Discovery of His Past: Literary Landmarks in Archaeology*. Englewood Cliffs: Prentice-Hall, 1962.

11. Herodotus, *The History*. Trans. David Greene. Chicago: University of Chicago Press, 1987.

12. Rebecca Cann, *et al.*, "Mitachondrial DNA and Human Evolution," *Nature*, 325, 1, January, 1987, pp. 31-36.

13. Maulana Karenga, *Kawaida Theory*. Los Angeles: Kawaida Press, 1980.

14. Cheikh Anta Diop, *Cultural Unity of Black Africa*. Chicago: Third World Press, 1976.

15. Rosalind Jeffries, "African Art and Its Continuities," Colgate University, October 18, 1988.

16. See K. Welsh-Asante, Special Issue on African American Dance, *Journal of Black Studies*, September 1985.

17. Alexander Pope, *Essay on Man*, Boston: Oliver and Munroe, 1951.

18. Stephen Jay Gould, *The Mismeasure of Man*. New York: Norton, 1981, p. 31.

19. Gould, p. 31.

20. James Chesebro, "Deconstructing Darwin's *Origin of the Species*," Speech Communication Association Conference, New Orleans, November 6, 1988.

21. Michael Bradley, *The Iceman Inheritance*. Toronto: Dorset, 1981.

22. Georg Hegel, *Reason in History*. Trans. R. Hortman. Indianapolis: Bobbs-Merrill, 1982, p. 3.

23. Hegel, p. 4.

24. Hegel, p. 9.

25. Hegel, p. 9.

26. Hegel, p. xxi.

27. Dona Richards, *Let the Circle Be Unbroken*. New York: DA Publishers, 1989. See also C. T. Keto's, *Africa-Centered Perspective on History*. Blackwood, NJ: K & A Publishers, 1989, for an extended version of the African cultural expression.

28. Edmund Husserl, *Ideas: General Introduction to (Pure) Phenomenology*. London: Alan and Unwin; New York: Macmillan, 1931.

29. Harold Garfinkel, *Studies in Ethnomethodology*. Englewood Cliffs: Prentice-Hall, 1967.

30. Kenneth Clarke, *Civilization: A Personal View*. New York: Harper and Row, 1969.

31. Adriano Vasco Rodrigues, *Historia Geral da Civilizacao*. Proto: Proto Editoria, 1968-69, p. 103.

32. Hegel, *Reason in History*, p. 3.

33. Hegel, p. 24.

34. Georg Hegel, *The Philosophy of History*. New York: Dover, 1956.

35. W. H. Walsh, "Principles and Prejudices in Hegel's Philosophy of History" in *Hegel's Political Philosophy: Problems and Perspectives*, edited by Z. A. Peltzynski. London: Cambridge University Press, 1971.

36. Hegel, *Philosophy*, p. 91.

37. Cheikh Anta Diop, *The African Origin of Civilization: Myth or Reality*. Westport, CT: Lawrence Hill, 1974.

38. Diop, p. 102.

39. Hegel, *Philosophy*, p. 96.

40. Karl Popper, "A Reply," in Imre Lakatos and Alan Musgrave, eds., *Criticism and the Growth of Knowledge*. London: Cambridge Univeristy Press, 1970.

41. Paul Feyerabend, *Against Method*. New York: Routledge, 1988.

42. Asante, *The Afrocentric Idea*. Philadelphia: Temple University Press, 1987.

43. Ivan Van Sertima, *They Came Before Columbus: The African Presence in the New World*. New York: Random House, 1976. This work combined history, botany, linguistics and anthropology to become an Africalogical study.

44. C. T. Keto, *The Africa Centered Perspective of History*. Blackwood, NJ: K. A. Publications, 1989, p. 15.

45. Keto, p. 15.

46. Keto, p. 15.

47. Lucius Outlaw, "Africology: Normative Theory" Symposium on Africology, Department of African American Studies, University of Wisconsin, Milwaukee, April 24, 1987, p. 42. At this symposium "Africology" was proposed as a new name for the discipline of Black Studies.

Part II   Anteriors

1. George F. Brooks, "A Provisional Historical Schema for Western Africa Based on Seven Climate Periods: ca. 9000 B.C. to the 19th Century," *Cahiers d'Etudes Africaines*, 101-102, XXVI-1-2, 1986, pp. 32-66.

2. Brooks, p. 46.

3. Brooks, p. 47.

4. See Basil Davidson, *The Lost Cities of Africa: African Genius*. Boston: Little Brown, 1959; Martin Bernal, *Black Athena*. New Brunswick: Rutgers University Press, 1987; and Maulana Karenga and Jacob Carruthers, eds., *Kemetic Worldview: Essays in Ancient Egyptian Studies*. Los Angeles: University of Sankore Press, 1984.

5. Eugen Strouhal, "Evidence of the Early Penetration of Negroes into Predynastic Egypt," *Journal of African History*, (1971) 12 (1), pp. 4-7.

6. Herodotus, *The History*. Chicago: University of Chicago Press, 1987.

7. Strouhal, p. 3.

8. Strouhal, p. 1.

9. Cheikh Anta Diop, "Histoire Primitive de L'Humanité Evolution du Monde Noir," *Bulletin de L'institut Francais d'Afrique Noire*, Ser. B, XXIV (1962), pp. 449-546.

10. G. Brunton and G. Caton-Thompson, *The Badarian Civilization and Predynastic Remains Near Badari*. London: Quaritch, 1928, pp. 40-42.

11. Strouhal, p. 7.

12. Albert Churchward, *The Signs and Symbols of Primordial Man*. Westport, CT: Greenwood Press, 1978.

13. Diop, *African Origins*.

14. Herodotus, *The History*, 2:50, p. 153.

15. This is not an arbitrary periodization but the results of thinking through the process of Egyptian culture based on an Afrocentric conceptualization.

16. Cheikh Anta Diop, *Parente genetique de l'Egyptien Pharaonique et des Langues Negro-Africaines*. Dakar: I.F.A.N., 1977; see also Maulana Karenga and Jacob Carruthers, *Kemetic Worldview: Essays in Ancient Egyptian Studies*. Los Angeles: University of Sankore Press, 1984.

17. Karenga and Carruthers, pp. 22-25.

18. Karenga and Carruthers, p. 22.

19. Carruthers, pp. 22-23.

20. Maulana Karenga, *The Husia*. Los Angeles: University of Sankore Press, 1984.

21. Ibn Khaldun, *The Muqaddimah: An Introduction to History*. Trans. Franz Rosenthal and ed. N. J. Dawood. Princeton: Princeton University Press, 1967.

22. Khaldun, *The Muqaddimah*.

23. E. E. Evans-Pritchard, *Essays in Social Anthropology*. New York: Free Press, 1963, p. 99.

24. Albert Hyma, *Ancient History*. Chicago: University of Chicago Press, 1965, p. 5.

25. Hyma, p. 8.

26. Hyma, p. 21.

27. Theophile Obenga, *Pour une nouvelle histoire*. Paris: Presence Africaine, 1980; Cheikh Anta Diop, *Precolonial Black Africa*. Paris: Presence Africaine, 1986.

28. Diodorus Siculus, *Histoire universelle*. Trans. Abbé Terrason. Book I:23, 2; Book I:60, Paris, 1758.

29. Plato, *Timaeus*, 22, 23.

30. Diogenes Laerce, *Thales*, 43, 24.

31. Jamblicus, *Life of Pythagoras*, 4:18-20.

32. Olympiodorus, *Life of Plato* and Strago, *Description of Egypt*, XVII, I, 29.

33. Maulana Karenga, *The Husia*. Los Angeles: University of Sankore Press, 1984.

34. James Breasted, *Development of Religion and Thought in Ancient Egypt*. London, 1912.

35. E.A.W. Budge, *The Egyptian Book of the Dead*. New York: Dover, 1967.

36. Budge, 1967, pp. xi-xxx.

37. Jacob Carruthers, *Essays in Ancient Egyptian Studies*. Los Angeles: University of Sankore Press, 1984.

38. Carruthers, p. 29.

39. Theophile Obenga, *Pour une Nouvelle Histoire*. Paris: Presence Africaine, 1980, p. 58.

40. This problem is not peculiar to graphic systems but relates to everything that deals with African knowledge and science. There was a concerted effort to separate Egypt from the rest of Africa in terms of philosophy, motif, science, religion, architecture, and language. Since the late 1950s the Diopian movement, initiated by the late Senegalese scientist Cheikh Anta Diop, has reasserted the organic relationship of ancient Egypt to the rest of Africa.

41. See the contemporary works of Maulana Karenga and Jacob Carruthers, *Kemet and the African Worldview*. Los Angeles: University of Sankore Press, 1986; and Jacob Carruthers, *Essays in Ancient Egyptian Studies*. Los Angeles: University of Sankore Press, 1984.

42. This position has been adequately explained by Theophile Obenga, *Pour une nouvelle Histoire*, Paris: Presence Africaine, 1980; by the life work of Cheikh Anta Diop, and especially in his posthumously published *Pre-Colonial Africa*. New York: Lawrence Hill, 1987.

43. The language of ancient Egypt is now being called "mdu neter," sacred words, by contemporary Kemetologists. Therefore, I have chosen to use the term "mdu" as the basic unit of the African script system. Although grapheme is normally used to mean the smallest single unit in a script, it is clearly Eurocentric bias of the idea of a script.

44. The Akan Sankofa system is based upon the tradition of Adinkra, a famous king of Gyaman, now Ivory Coast. Adinkra angered Asantehene Bonsu-Panyin by trying to copy the Golden Stool. Adinkra was slain in a war with the Asantehene. The term "Sankofa" is often used to refer to the Adinkra symbols but Sankofa is only one of the symbols. Adinkra means literally "good-bye" or "farewell."

45. The Association for the Study of Classical African Civilizations has legislated the use of mdu netr or medu neters, sacred language, to identify ancient Egyptian.

46. Nsibidi may exist as a proto-generator of symbolic systems by virtue of the confluence of cultures and ideas in the region of its origin.

47. G. Kubik, "African Graphic Systems," *Muntu*, vol. 1, no. 4-5, 1986.

48. G. Kubik, "African Graphic Systems: A Reassessment," *Mitteilungan der Anthropologischen Gesellscraft in Wien*, vols. 114 and 115, 1984-1985. E. Jaritz. "Uber Bahnen auf Billardtischen-Oder: Eine Mathematische Untersuchung von Ideogrammen Angolanischer Herkunft," Mathematisch-Statistiche Sektion, Research Centre A-8010, Graz, Austria, 1983.

49. Mathematics finds its source in Africa. The Egyptians have been shown to have discovered the use of zero long before the Indians or the Chinese. Such discoveries may have originated with the migration journeys of many ancient clans and groups. As the hunters and other stopped to rest they often played numerical games. It is possible that out of such leisure activity, the first African thinkers created mathematics.

50. G. Niangoran-Bouah, *L'univers Akan des Poids a Peser L'or*. Abidjan: Les Nouvelles Editions Africaines, 1984.

51. Niangoran-Bouah, *L'univers*,

52. Niangoran-Bouah,

53. Niangoran-Bouah,

54. Niangoran-Bouah,

55. Kubik, *African Graphic Systems*, 1986, p. 78.

56. Theophile Obenga, *L'Afrique dans l'Antiquité: Egypte Pharaonique-African Noire*. Paris: Presence Africaine, 1973, p. 371.

57. Kubik, 1986.

58. Kubik, 1986.

59. Hyma, *Ancient History*, 1965.

60. See particularly Marie-Louise Bastin, *Art Decoratif Ishokwe*. Lisboa, 1961; Maurice De La Fosse, "Les Vai, leur Langue et leur Systeme d'écriture," *L'Anthropologie*, X, 1899; C. A. Gollmer, "On African Symbolic Messages," *Journal of the Anthropological Institute*, XIV, 1885; Louise Jefferson, *The Decorative Arts of Africa*. New York: Collins, 1972; M. Kibanda, "L'écriture dans la civilisation Kongo: Problemes theoriques et methodologiques," *Revue de Linguistique Theorique et Appliquee*, Janvier, 1985; and A. K. Quarcoo, *The Language of Adinkra Patterns*. Legon: University of Ghana, Institute of African Studies, 1972.

61. Cheikh Anta Diop, *Parente genetique de L'Egyptien Pharaonique et des langues Negro-Africaine*. Dakar: I.F.A.N., Les Nouvelles Editions Africaines, 1977, p. xxv.

62. Diop, p. xxv.

63. Diop, *Parente Genetique.*
64. Preiswerk and Perrot, *Ethnocentrism in History.* New York: NOK Publishers, 1974, p. 97.
65. Maulana Karenga, *The Husia.* Los Angeles: University of Sankore Press, 1984, p. xiv.
66. Henri Frankfort, *Ancient Egyptian Religion.* New York: Harper and Row, 1961, p. 81.
67. Dona Richards, "The Implications of African American Spirituality" in M. Asante and K. W. Asante, *African Culture: The Rhythms of Unity.*
68. *Ibid.,* p. 210.
69. Robert Lawlor, "Preface" in R. A. Schwaller de Lubicz, *Symbol and the Symbolic.* New York: Inner Traditions, 1978, p. 17.
70. *Ibid.,* p. 15.
71. R. A. Schwaller de Lubicz, *Symbolic and the Symbolic.* New York: Inner Traditions, 1978.
72. Marcel Griaule, *Conversations with Ogotemmeli.* New York: Oxford University Press, 1978.
73. Wole Soyinka, "The Ethno-Cultural Debate" in *African Culture: The Rhythms of Unity.*
74. Niangoran-Bouah, *L'univers.*
75. Albert Churchward, *The Signs and Symbols of Primordial Man.* Westport, CT: Greenwood Press, 1978, p. xvi.
76. Churchward, 1978, p. 2.
77. Churchward, p. 3.
78. Churchward, p. 8.
79. Martin Bernal, *Black Athena.* New Brunswick: Rutgers University Press, 1987, pp. 51-52.
80. Bernal, p. 52.
81. Bernal, p. 52.
82. Bernal, p. 203.
83. Bernal, p. 152.
84. Bernal, p. 153.
85. Bernal, p. 154.
86. Wade Nobles, *African and African American Cultural Blueprint/ Framework for Black Family Pilot Project.* Oakland: Institute for the Advanced Study of the Black Family, 1988, p. 1.
87. R. Horton, *Kalabar: Sculpture.* Lagos, 1965, pp. 5-6.
88. Denis Williams, *Icon and Image.* New York: New York University Press, 1974, p. 19.
89. Wade Nobles and Lawrence Goddard, "Analytical Model of Human Functioning," Oakland: Institute for the Advanced Study of the Black Family, 1988, p. 1.
90. J. Piaget, *Structuralism.* New York: Basic, 1970.

91. Piaget, p. 5.
92. Kariamu Welsh-Asante, "Commonalities in African Dance: An Aesthetic Foundation for African Dance" in (eds.) M. Asante and K. W. Asante, *African Culture: Rhythms of Unity.*
93. Sigmund Freud, *Civilization and Its Discontents.*
94. Roy Preiswerk and Dominique Perrot, *Ethnocentrism in History.* New York: NOK, 1977, p. xvi.
95. William Simmons, *Men of Mark.* New York: Arno Press, 1968, p. 1007.
96. Edward Wilmot Blyden, *Christianity, Islam and the Negro Race.* Edinburgh: Edinburgh University Press, 1967. See particularly pp. 1-45.
97. Holis Lynch, *Black Spokesman.* New York: Humanities Press, 1971, p. xxxi.
98. Lynch, p. 9.
99. Al-Amin Mazrui, *The African Condition.* London: Heinemann, 1980, p. xi.
100. Hailu Habtu, "The Fallacy of the 'Triple Heritage' Thesis: A Critique," *Issue,* 1984, vol. XIII, p. 26.
101. Habtu, p. 26.
102. Habtu, p. 27.
103. These are not the only African Americans engaged in the new historiography. One finds a considerable interest among graduate students at Temple University and Cornell University where student organizations have been formed to advance the intellectual tradition begun by Diop. The Imhotep order at Temple sponsors the publication, *Imhotep: An Afrocentric Review,* which contains articles in the Afrocentric circle.
104. Ngugi Wa Thiong'o, *Decolonising the Mind.* London: Heinemann, 1986, p. 4.
105. Ngugi, p. 4.
106. Ngugi, p. 18.
107. Ngugi, *Decolonising the Mind.*
108. Ngugi, p. 3.
109. Chinweizu, *Decolonizing the African Mind.* London: Sundoor, 1989.
110. John Jackson, *Introduction to African Civilizations.* Secausus, NJ: Citadel Press, 1974, pp. 158-159.
111. Harry Johnston, *The Uganda Protectorate,* London, Vol. II, p. 473.
112. Herodotus, *The History,* 2:91-93, pp. 168-169.
113. J. C. DeGraft-Johnson, *African Glory,* p. 25.
114. Edward Said, *Orientalism.* New York: Vintage, 1979, p. 3.
115. Said, *Orientalism,* p. 3.
116. Said, p. 6.
117. Said, p. 11.

118. Said, p. 17.
119. Said, p. 53.
120. Said, p. 22.
121. Said, p. 137.
122. Said, p. 50.
123. Said, p. 81.
124. Said, p. 82.
125. Jean-Baptiste-Joseph Fourier, *Preface Historique, Description de Egypte*. Paris, 1810.
126. Sulayman Nyang, *Islam, Christianity and African Identity*. Brattleboro, VT: Amana, 1984, p. 9.
127. Nyang, p. 20.
128. Nyang, p. 29.
129. Nyang, p. 29.
130. Nyang, p. 48.
131. Nyang, p. 48.
132. MacMichael, 1967, p. 4.
133. MacMichael, p. 12.
134. MacMichael, p. 14.
135. MacMichael, p. 16.
136. MacMichael, p. 21.
137. MacMichael, p. 29.
138. MacMichael, p. 29.
139. MacMichael, p. 31.
140. Basil Davidson, *Lost Cities of Africa*. Boston: Little, Brown and Company, 1959, pp. 7-45.
141. Churchward, *The Signs and Symbols of Primordial Man*, p. 214.
142. Ibn Khaldun, *The Muqaddimah: An Introduction to History*. Princeton: Princeton University Press, 1967, p. 63.
143. Khaldun, p. 63.
144. Khaldun, p. 64.
145. David W. Phillipson, *African Archaeology*. London: Cambridge University Press, 1985, p. 3.
146. Phillipson, p. 6.
147. Preiswerk and Perrot, p. xxi.
148. Preiswerk and Perrot, p. xxi.
149. Jan Vansina, *Oral Tradition*. Madison: University of Wisconsin Press, 1965.
150. Phillipson, p. 13.
151. Linda Brodkey, *Academic Writing as Social Practice*. Philadelphia: Temple University Press, 1987, pp. 20-21.
152. Brodkey, p. 21.
153. Brodkey, p. 88.

154. Dona Richards, "Progress and the European Concept of Domination," *Contemporary Black Thought*, (eds.) M. Asante and A. Vandi. Beverly Hills: Sage Publications, 1981.

155. Karenga, *Kawaida Theory*, p. 18.

156. Karenga, p. 18.

157. Preiswerk and Perrot, pp. 4-5.

158. Charshee McIntyre.

159. Preiswerk and Perrot, p. 13.

160. Preiswerk and Perrot, p. 34.

161. Preiswerk and Perrot, pp. 35-36.

162. Preiswerk and Perrot, p. 37.

163. Preiswerk and Perrot, pp. 37-38. Communicationists have examined conversation, discourse, and media from intercultural angles since the 1970s. However, the rewards of cosmocultural conceptions based on the centrism without hierarchy of all cultures should open up a more equitable human communication paradigm. See also Molefi Asante, Eileen Newmark and Cecil Blake (eds.), *Handbook of Intercultural Communication*. Beverly Hills: Sage Publications, 1979. An update of this volume published in 1989 is edited by Molefi Asante and William Gudykunst, *Handbook of International and Intercultural Communication*.

164. Preiswerk and Perrot, p. 40.

165. Preiswerk and Perrot, p. 40.

166. Preiswerk and Perrot, p. 44. In fact, in November, 1988, a group of nearly three hundred American scholars, including one black English professor from Duke University, gathered in New York to reinforce their monocultural commitment. For them, "cultural domination" was an essentially natural phenomenon. The corollary happens to be the stifling of other views; such a position is not only anti-thetical to the democratic ideal, it virtually assures a factionalized society.

167. Preiswerk and Perrot, p. 44.

168. See especially, Jack Daniel (ed.), *Black Communication*. New York: SCA, 1970.

169. Preiswerk and Perrot, p. 46.

Part III Exteriors

1. Carter G. Woodson, *The Mis-education of the Negro*. Washington: Associated Publishers, 1933, p. 7.

2. Woodson, p. 1.

3. Woodson, p. 134.

4. Woodson, p. 96.

5. Woodson, p. 23.

6. Ralph Ellison, *Invisible Man*. New York: Random House, 1952.

7. MacIntyre, *Marxism and Christianity*. New York: Shocken Books, 1968, pp. 37-43.

8. MacIntyre, p. 31.

9. Walter Rodney, *How Europe Underdeveloped Africa*. Washington: Howard University Press, 1980.

10. Frantz Fanon, *Black Skins, White Masks*. New York: Grove, 1967.

11. David Caute, *Frantz Fanon*. New York: Viking Press, p. 2.

12. James Baldwin, *The Fire Next Time*. New York: Dial, 1964, p. 16.

13. Frantz Fanon, *The Wretched of the Earth*. New York: Grove Press, 1965, p. 252.

14. Fanon, *The Wretched*.

15. Fanon, *The Wretched*. See Jean Paul Sartre's Preface, pp. 18-19.

16. Fanon, *Black Skin*, p. 81.

17. John Henrik Clarke, "The Black Man's History in a White Man's World." Speech given at City College, September, 1983.

18. Karl Jung, *Symbols and Transformation*. Princeton: Princeton University Press, 1961.

19. Frank Tucker, *The White Conscience*. New York: Frederick Ungar Publishing Co., 1968.

20. Tucker, *The White Conscience*.

21. Lewis Hanke, *The Spanish Struggle for Justice in the Conquest of the Americas*. Philadelphia, 1949; Lewis Hanke, *Aristotle and the American Indians*. Chicago, 1959.

22. Hanke, *The Spanish Struggle*, p. 73.

23. Edward O. Wilson, *On Human Nature*. Cambridge: Harvard University Press, 1978, p. 167.

24. A. Rosenberg, *Sociobiology and the Preemption of Social Science*. Baltimore: John Hopkins University Press, 1980.

25. Arthur Lovejoy, *Great Chain of Being*. New York: Harper and Row, 1960.

26. Josiah A. Cobbah, "African Values and the Human Rights Debate: An African Perspective," *Human Rights Quarterly*, 9, 1987, pp. 309-331.

27. Cobbah, p. 310.

28. Edward Allen Kent, "Taking Human Rights Seriously," in *Rationality in Thought and Action*, (eds.) Martin Tammy and K. D. Irani. New York: Greenwood Press, 1986, p. 37.

29. Abdias do Nascimento, *Mixture or Massacre: The Genocide of a People*. Buffalo: Afrodiaspora, 1978; and Michael Omi and Howard Winant, *Racial Formation in the United States*. New York: Routledge, 1986.

30. Elisa Nascimento, *Pan Africanism and South America*. Buffalo: Afrodiaspora, 1979, p. 6.

31. Nascimento, p. 6.

32. Amos Wilson, "African American Social and Cultural Affirmation," Temple University, May 6, 1988.

33. Ronald Walters, "Marxism-Leninism and Black Revolution," *Black Books Bulletin*, 5:3, Fall.

34. John Blassingame, *The Slave Community*. New York: Oxford University Press, 1972, p. 2.

35. Vincent Harding, *There is a River*. New York: Harcourt, Brace, Jovanovich, 1981.

36. Stuckey, pp. 11-46.

Subject Index

Name Index _____